Splashes of Life

Based on a Collection of Real-Life Short Stories Depicting

the Years 1920-1949

By

Fanny Louise Smith

This book is a work of fiction. Places, events, and situations in this story are purely fictional. Any resemblance to actual persons, living or dead, is coincidental.

ISBN: 0-7596-9312-9 (e-book)
ISBN: 0-7596-9313-7 (Paperback)

This book is printed on acid free paper.

1stBooks - rev. 06/11/02

In dedication and loving memory to my children and their children and to the ages to come. And to my dear mother to whom so bravely bore the burden of raising eight children to fruition alone, during what is known as the Great Depression.

Where is your self to be found? Always in the deepest enchantment that you have experienced.

By Hofmannsthal

INDEX

PART ONE

YEARS 1920-1935

Fanny Louise Smith

THE PRICELESS BILLY GOAT

As children we talked and talked about goats and how we'd like to have one for a pet, knowing very well mom had enough mouths to feed and wouldn't consider having one. There was no way she'd consider having a goat, especially a male goat, because it could not produce milk. And yet, goats were one of my favorite animals. Mostly because I liked to see them leap, jump, hop, bounce, and run so fast.

Around 1920 radios were invented, and most people were astonished at how voices came through little boxes. The voices were loud and clear, and one man decided to find out how voices came through the box. One day he took his radio apart, and laid the pieces on a table so he could look them over one at a time to see what caused the voices to come through. After looking each piece over it was still a puzzle to him. He was one of the few people who had a phone, so he called his neighbor who had a phone to come to his house to look at the inside of his radio. Phones then were the cranking kind, and most people were on party lines. Anyone on his party-could listen in on the conversation. Shortly after calling his neighbor, four men came to his house excited about the radio he had taken apart. Two of the men didn't own a radio and they really were excited about seeing the inside of a radio. It seemed so amazing to them. After looking every little part over carefully, they sat around for hours discussing how a voice could come through the box.

Back then your neighbors who didn't have a radio would come to your house to listen to it with you. Some of them got so involved in the program you would have thought they were in the program.

One day after our chores were done, we were glued to the radio like people are today to their television sets or computers. Out of the blue came a loud, clear voice, saying: Ned Jones, who lives on Opossum Trot Road, has a goat he can't keep any longer. Anyone interested should come to see it. My two sisters and I were utterly surprised when the radio said it was Ned Jones who lived near us. How amazing! We had wanted a goat for so very long. How wonderful it would be for us to get this real live goat.

Out of mom's sight, we put our heads to work. We had to figure a way to convince mom how fantastic it would be to have this goat. Chatting away trying to find a solution, we decided we'd ask mom if we could go play with Ned Jones' girl for a while. Since Ned Jones lived a short distance from us, she gave us permission to play there for one hour.

More than anything else in our whole life, after we saw this goat, we just had to have him. Now, how were we going to convince mom how very wonderful a goat would be to play with and have as a real pet. Surely, a goat would be better than a cat, dog, or even a horse. Just to see this wonderful goat made us jump and bounce around with joy.

IMAGINE THIS! Mrs. Jones actually called this goat, BILLY. What a wonderful name for a goat.

We proceeded to talk and talk to Ned Jones to convince him it would be okay with our mom to take Billy. Finally he said, "Tell you what. If all of you children will weed my garden you can take Billy home." We hurried to weed Mr. Jones' garden as fast as we could, we really did, although it was hard to keep our minds on weeding while watching Billy. At last we finished weeding the garden. We tried to stay calm while Ned Jones got the goat for us. As soon as possible we wanted to get our Billy home.

You'd think it would be easy to get a goat to go the way you need it to. But just try it sometimes and you'll see they never ever go where you want them to. Billy was stronger then all three of us put together! He sure was! Can't you just see us three girls struggling to get him to where we wanted him to go while he was dead set and determined to go the way he wanted to go. It's just the way goats are. They are as stubborn as any mule you will ever meet.

Since we wanted our mom to like Billy, we didn't want to be late getting home. Mom wanted us home in one hour and she always expected us to follow her orders. Getting this goat home fast had become a royal battle but convincing mom to keep it when we got there, would be a whole other story. I figured we'd have to do some mighty fast talking for her to say, "yes."

You should have seen us pushing, pulling, and grabbing Billy's ears. He knocked us aside as if we were pieces of paper. We screamed and yelled at him to no avail; nothing seemed to work. There was not much time left, but that didn't stop us from laughing and laughing all the way. Everything seemed so funny as we struggled. Yet Billy insisted on going his own way regardless of what we did to try and make him go the way we wanted him to go. We were having the time of our lives, laughing until tears came to our eyes, and even that was funny to us. Certain of our activities with the goat could have been made into a movie, I was sure. Except back then, there were only silent movies; this one needed voices.

Billy thought he was going to outdo us or get the best of us. But there was no way he was going to do that, because we were dead set and determined to get Billy home.

We tried to conquer him by hanging onto his horns and ears, but that didn't work. So all three of us did some serious discussing on how to get Billy home. Certainly if we pleaded with him, he would come with us. But he paid us no attention. He acted like he didn't even belong to us! We thought if we told him how nice he was and do some sweet talking to him, he would listen. But he didn't pay any attention to that either.

Man! Oh, man! Can you believe this goat? This goat really was getting disgusting now. We decided to try one more thing. Maybe we could get hold of his stubby tail while two of us held his horns tightly, and then whisper in his ear how he belonged to us now and had to come with us real peaceful.

Can you believe it? We didn't talk him into anything. We were really puzzled at what our next move would be. We simply had to find a way to persuade him to come along without knocking us around. The way he was bouncing us around we could have broken some bones.

Since we were in a hurry now, there had to be some way we could persuade this ridiculous goat to come along quickly. We decided to yell at him and command him to come along with us peacefully. We had already told him how we would take the very best care of him and how sweet and nice he was. Now our patience was gone, and we yelled and screamed to let him really know who was boss.

He was so sweet at times, but now it was time to get serious. Watching him, we didn't know what to do until we saw him starting to nibble on some clover and some grass. All of a sudden my sister said, "What about getting some nice grass for him." If he likes it, then we can lure him toward our house with it.

To us this was unbelievably easy. He came along following the grass at his mouth just as nice as you please. Then we ran. He stopped just before we got home, standing there looking high and mighty. He seemed to know what he was doing. He wouldn't go another step until we let him eat some of the grass. When it was gone, he turned and started marching back toward his home. What a disaster! Time was running out for us. Thinking quickly, we decided to have one of us get on his back. But under no circumstances was he going to let anyone get on his back. Then two of us pulled on his laid back horns while the other one pushed as hard as she could. After he had bounced us around giving us more cuts and bruises, our last solution was to get more

5

fresh clover and pretend we were eating it right in front of him. Anyway he turned his head, we would stay right in front of him. You'd think that was easy to do. Not the way we were doing it. He didn't like it. Disgusted and bewildered, we sat down thinking that perhaps if we paid no attention to him, maybe he would get lonely. Suddenly, he came over to us and again we got the very best clover and grass we could find. Again we held it in front of him just enough out of reach so he would have to follow us to get at it. We went faster and faster until we finally got home.

We tied him securely to a hickory nut tree and let him take turns knocking us down. With all the commotion, mom came to the door just in time to see Billy butt me down. Wish you could have seen the look on mom's face. She was one surprised mom! She couldn't believe her eyes. Loudly she said, "Just how did you get that old smelly goat?

Mom was not at all happy about our priceless Billy. She told us to take it right back. I said, Oh mom! "It's dark now. Can we please keep him until morning?" Waiting anxiously with our heads down, tears were starting to flow. Again we begged, "Please, please, please mom, let us keep him!" She paused, as if thinking about it, while each one of us all at once tried to tell her how fantastic Billy truly was. She avoided saying anything for a few more minutes. Finally in our last effort to persuade mom, we told her we would feed, water, bathe, and stay with him all day long. And she wouldn't have to do a single thing to care for him. We pleaded with her, telling her how wonderful Billy really was and if she would only give us and Billy one chance.

Just about the time we were about to give up, mom said, "Okay, let's try it out for a while and see how it goes." If only you could have seen us bouncing and jumping around with pure joy, just to think we got our way and won the battle.

The next day, all three of us played all day with our priceless Billy, gleefully watching him bounce, hop, jump, and leap over things. We loved to watch him kick his hoofs up toward the sky, as if he was going to fly. Suddenly, us girls, decided to go into the house for awhile. Of course Billy, who was right on our heels, came right in with us, as if he owned the place.

Once inside, there was not one thing he touched in which was not totally demolished. He went from one place to another, destroying everything in his pathway. It was a disaster, a total mess. We pushed, pulled, yanked, screamed, and yelled at him, but we could not get him out of the house. No way! In desperation we yelled at the top of our voices, calling him a smelly old goat. He jumped on top of the table and looked around as innocent as you please. Oh, how sweet he appeared. Did he know what a disaster he made inside the house? He looked so intelligent and important with his head held high, looking us right in the eyes. Yes, I do believe he knew what a disaster he had caused, and he was daring us to get him off the table.

We hurried to get him some real nice clover to entice him to jump off the table. We absolutely had to get him off the table and out of th house before mom came in from the garden. And we had to clean up the mess super good before mom saw it. Billy came along following us as we put the sweet clover in front of his mouth. We let him nibble some, than we walked him into the back yard, going as fast as we could. The three of us were running and Billy was right behind us. Once he stopped and stood with his head high as if he were some kind of king, prince, or big shot. We realized he knew he was an intelligent goat. But what a mess we had to get cleaned up quickly if we wanted to keep our priceless goat.

After everything was kind of cleaned up and the broken dishes hidden, we decided to play outside with Billy. Of course, we closed the door very tightly behind us. We had enough of cleaning up. You betcha!

The very first thing we did was to show our Billy the large muddy water puddle in the back yard. Talk about a mistake, this was a BIG MISTAKE!

I decided this would be an easy place to get on his back for a nice ride. BOY! Oh, boy! What a ride it was. He leaped, bounced, hopped, jumped, and ran as fast as he could just to buck me off. I'm sure he knew exactly what he was doing. Off I went with a, BANG. I jumped up, laughing as hard as I could. You can't imagine how much fun this was, as he threw me off time after time. Since it was so much fun, I decided to get on his laid back horns for another good ride. It was totally unreal. He held his horns high with me on them and lowered his head running all the while, than he gave me a heave ho. Up and out I went, falling to the ground in a heap. I rode him again and again and each time I landed in a different position. He would stand there with a twinkle in his eye as if he knew exactly what he was doing and how much fun it was to do it.

Now he hopped, leaped, jumped, and ran as fast as possible until he got to a mud puddle. Then, he stopped suddenly just to throw me into the mud puddle. It was really a total shock at first, then I realized it was loads and loads of fun. GOLLY! GEE! Could anyone have more fun than this. I wiped the mud out of my eyes so I could see, and spit the mud out of my mouth.

It was about time for my two sisters to have this kind of fun too. Just as he had me, Billy dumped each one of them in the mud in different landing positions. You should have seen us rolling on the ground and bouncing around screaming with laughter.

We yelled out saying, "LORDIE MERCY! Do let us have this kind of fun forever and ever, please."

In a little while we decided to let Billy rest. He just stood there for a few minutes with a sparkle in his eye and a grin on his face. I'm sure he was waiting for us to get on him again so he could dump us in the middle of the mud puddle. OH! What a goat!

Now we really knew our Billy was priceless. Nothing or no one was going to deprive us of our Billy! WHOA! WAIT! Oh, yeah! There was mom to consider.

Wondering what the commotion was outside, mom decided to come out to the backyard to see for herself. MAN! Oh, man! What a mess she beheld. There was not one spot of clean flesh nor clean clothes on any of us. We were nothing but mud cakes from head to toe.

With our heads down, we stood very still while mom looked us over. Mom wasn't one bit happy with us. But why? Didn't she want us to have fun? It didn't help matters that Billy was strutting around with his head held high like he was a Prince, or big shot. We didn't think it was so awful for Billy to throw us in the mud puddle. After all it was good clean dirt.

The way mom was eyeing us, I didn't figure mom appreciated our Billy the same as we did. Nor did she understand how we felt. Mom just plain let us know right off what a mess we were in and she actually yelled at our Billy. She called him a smelly old goat. Of all the things to say, that was the worst. Our poor Billy had to endure hearing such a thing. For no good reason at all, she said, We had to get rid of Billy.

We tried desperately to think of a good solution for this horrible problem as soon as possible. The first thing we thought of was to hide him in our bedroom. Surely he would sleep some of the time, and the rest of the time we could try to keep him quiet. Then we remembered his activities of leaping around and knocking things over. NO!

That would never do. Then we thought about taking him behind some bushes, out of mom's sight. But sure as anything he would BAAAA, as loud as he could, knowing he was out there behind the bushes all by himself, and he'd be so very lonely because he loves to be with us to much. Maybe we could take him to a ditch. NO! That would never do. We couldn't get down in the ditch easily and there was nothing to tie him to in the ditch. Besides what about feeding and watering him? Besides, sliding down in the ditch would leave us dirty and mom would know something wasn't right. Forget that!

Or maybe we could take him over to our neighbor. But we didn't think that would work either since the first thing Billy would do would be to knock over everything in his pathway, and that would make a one very unhappy neighbor.

The way mom said to get rid of Billy, we knew she would take no fooling around about it. We knew we had to get rid of him as soon as possible. Why didn't mom understand children? Even though it broke our hearts, we tried our best to find Billy a new home, as mom wanted. We talked to anyone we saw to tell them what a fantastic goat Billy was. But no one seemed to understand how great he was or to appreciate how he acted like a king, Prince, or a big shot of some kind.

We never mentioned to anyone what a disaster he had caused in our kitchen, how hard it was to get him off the table, or about the terrible mess we had to clean up after he was through. We tried and tried to get rid of our priceless Billy, but met with no success. One thing was for sure, we did not want to displease our wonderful mom.

Finally, a boy who lived on Turkey Run Road came to our house to look at Billy. Guess what? He fell in love with Billy. Of course, we only told him all the good things Billy could do. We didn't tell him about how he practically destroyed our house or how he enjoyed dumping us in a mud puddle. We didn't think he was going to take him, so we offered him a rope and told him how to hold good grass in front of his nose to get him to follow you wherever you should want to take him. He started to rub Billy's head, and Billy then pretended to butt him. This boy from Turkey Run Road thought it was so funny, it didn't take him long too fall in love with Billy. He said, "You have one wonderfully smart goat and I just can't leave without him." We made an agreement with him to take his bicycle which was to large for us at the moment, but we would grow into it soon.

By the time we grew large enough to ride the old bicycle, the tires were rotten. But, we certainly couldn't complain about the trade because our priceless goat did get a loving home. The boy from Turkey Run Road loved our Billy. We were sure of that! We knew for sure we would never have as much fun again in our whole lives without our one and only goat. If it were

9

not for the muddy puddle and the smelly goat smell, we might still have our priceless Billy.

THE OLD OUTHOUSE

Although there are many things wrong with outhouses, believe me they are better than nothing when you need to relieve yourself in a big hurry. You know what I mean by a rushing kind of hurry. In the old days most people had outhouses not far from their back door. One of the most obvious problems was that it would fill up after a few years of use. Of course, the more *Sears and Roebuck* catalog pages used, the faster the outhouse hole would fill up.

The older members of our family would read the catalog while doing their business and look at items they wanted to order. My sister Beth and I could not read many of the words, so we would look at the black and white pictures and pretend we could order out of the old catalog too. It was hard for us to look at the catalog and do our business. We would lay the catalog on the floor and turn the pages to where the toys were and look, look, and look, trying to decide which toy we would like to have the most. The outhouse holes were a little to large for us. We had to hold on tight too keep from falling in.

Somehow when you have brothers older than you, they like to scare the BLANK out of you. What a good time my brothers had scaring the you-know-what out of us. OH! YEAH! It was a delight for them to capture and kill a snake, and then lay it in a good striking position in the outhouse with a sliver of wood to hold it's mouth wide open so that it looked alive and as if it was going to strike and bite you. Just imagine opening the door in a mighty big hurry to do your business that simply cannot wait. It's horrifying to say the least!

Another trick they liked to play was to search for the biggest, blackest scorpions they could find. They'd paint a straight pin black, stick it in the largest part of the scorpions body, and pin it on a white piece of paper. Of course, they would place the scorpion right inside the outhouse door. Hoooooooly cow! When opening the door to rush in to do your business, can you imagine your reaction? We would scream and run out, trying to hold our urgent business until we could find a place to get relief. My brothers Tim and Monte, hiding nearby, would laugh until they cried.

Although the old outhouse was about ready to fall down, was almost full, and didn't have much space to move in it, our brothers didn't think it should be torn down. Their little sisters knew exactly why they didn't want the old outhouse torn down and a new one built. I'll tell you why, because the new one would have more room in it, and there would be too much space to be scared half to death. They tried to talk mom into not tearing the old outhouse down, but to no avail.

Mom wanted the new outhouse built before Uncle George and Aunt Lucy came from up north to visit us for a week or two. Somehow, it didn't quiet happen that way. George and Lucy were coming to help mom, because Papa had left her with four young children to raise. Mom never wanted anyone to help her, being an independent, help-yourself kind of person. One of her sayings was: "Be independent. Don't depend on others." Or: "If you want it done right, do it yourself. Ask for as little from others as you can." Even though she needed help to build the new outhouse before winter, she hated to accept help.

Mom got word her brother George and his wife would be arriving in one month. Each one of us was doing all we could to get things ready for them. Uncle George and Aunt Lucy, who lived in Washington D.C., wanted a longer stay, but they had to be back on the first of August. It would take them over a month to get to where we lived in Alabama. They would be in Alabama for two weeks.

Finally the day came when they arrived early one morning. They had been traveling since daybreak and were very tired and covered with dust. The last part of their trip had been by a two-horse buggy. Aunt Lucy's big hat and fine lace trim dress were covered with dust. She stepped out of the buggy, trying to dust off. She said, "I've never been so dirty anywhere."

Uncle George was a tall, well-built, distinguished, dominant type of person. Anyone could tell by the way he talked, walked, and looked at you. If Aunt Lucy talked too much, Uncle George would say to her, "Now, now Lucy. You know women should be seen and not heard." Behind his back she would talk up a blue streak. She could really talk and talk. I guess it was because she couldn't talk when he was present.

Aunt Lucy told us, she was a city girl but loved all the beautiful trees and flowers in the South, especially the birds.

They had brought in some packages and we would not dare ask what was in those packages. We knew better. Before evening Uncle George asked Lucy to bring out the packages. Quickly he opened them. He'd brought each of us one gift. My brothers, Tim and Monte's gift, was a miniature iron horse. And Beth's and mine were beautiful China doll's. We had never dreamed we would be able to have such a beautiful thing. To top that off, with a great big grin on his face, he pulled out of his carrying case a little leather sack heavy with gold pieces. He must have had a dozen or more, and he handed mom one of the twenty-dollar gold pieces. We were in total shock. We had been poor for a long time, and that was a mighty sum of money back then.

The first day Aunt Lucy kept going to the rickety old outhouse. Late the next morning, she stormed out of it angrily and refused to use the our old outhouse anymore. I think I know why. Could it be my brothers had pulled one of their awful tricks on her. I'll betcha' they did.

She didn't say anything to Uncle George about it. I'm sure she didn't want him to know, because he would get riled up for sure. Uncle George could not understand Lucy's attitude when she complained, saying, "I refuse to go in that old outhouse again. George will you give another twenty-dollar gold piece so you can build them a new outhouse?"

By this time, Aunt Lucy was set on leaving. Mom pleaded with her to stay and offered her the best bed chamber they had. A bed chamber is a pot with a lid that is used when it is rainy or to cold outside. When morning comes, it's emptied in the outhouse. Even though our outhouse was about full of you-know-what, surely it could hold a few more chambers full of the stuff, we thought. More than anything, we wanted them to stay a little longer, even if the outhouse was full.

When full of people, our house was the happiest house you will ever see. And just think, we would soon have a new, bigger outhouse. There would be enough room in the new outhouse for the two *Sears and Roebuck* catalogs and even room to spare. A special hook would be added for hanging pants on, and also a fancy mirror. Can you imagine how lucky we felt.

Mom wanted pictures of the old outhouse to give her brother George. Grabbing her old brownie camera, she told us to line up near the outhouse. Just as she got us in focus, we jumped back behind the outhouse. When she got ready to take the next picture, we knew better than to try that trick again.

We were all so delighted to know that soon we would have a new outhouse. YES! SIREE! My brothers even promised they would help build and keep the new outhouse clean so they would have a wonderful place to go pooh-pooh! We'll wait and see won't we.

Now mom did have the two gold pieces to build a fancy outhouse. The door would be prettier and better than any one for miles around. There would be enough money left for some new furniture and material for new school dresses. Tim and Monte would be able to get boots and a rifle to hunt wild game for meat. They could not contain themselves. They had never dreamed

13

of having money for the things they wanted most. This outhouse was going to be something to be very proud of. We might even have enough to paint the new outhouse. How lucky can a person be.

Mom could have hired help, but there was no way it would be considered in our family when we could do the work ourselves. Also, when there is a goal in mind, it makes you fell better if you accomplish it yourself.

Tim and Monte worked digging the six-by-six foot hole, five feet deep in a hurry.

They sang a song about going to the nicest outhouse in the state, because it was your fate, and on and on about pooh-poohing in the outhouse, and so forth. Mom was busy cutting the nice smooth boards she had bought for the seat. Beth watched and tried to help now and then. Looking at the holes mom made, we could not believe our eyes. There were two large ones but only one small hole. Didn't mom know the large ones were much too big for us and we'd surely fall butt first completely through the hole and disappear forever. Five foot down seemed a long way for us to fall. What if Beth and I had to go at the same time? What in the world would we do with only one small hole? Maybe she was making us only one hole because we had been too pesky at times.

The old outhouse was soon torn down and the new one stood finished in its place. It shone like one of the twenty-dollar gold pieces that had made it possible to build. It did shine all right, with orange paint.

Beth could hardly wait to go to school for the first time. She was as proud as a strutting peacock because she would be wearing her new shoes. Beth was a small six-year old and about as frisky as can be. Her teacher, Ms. Smith, said she would come to see her. She was required to go to each student's home to talk to the mother and see for herself her student's living conditions. I told Beth not to worry, that she does this every year. Ms. Smith had been to our home last year and the year before.

There was lots of excitement around our house getting things in perfect condition so the teacher could see what a wonderful family we were. Beth bounced all over the place trying to help. She wanted her new shoes placed where the teacher could see them first. She decided to put them on our very best chair, the chair the teacher would sit in.

In our household we were taught to respect our shoes because money was hard to come by. Mom required everyone to take their shoes off the minute they got home from school to save wear and tear on them. She always bought our shoes one-half size to large so we wouldn't outgrow them so fast. Beth took hog lard and rubbed it on her shoes to make them shine. She could hardly wait for the teacher to see her new shoes.

The next morning all of us were happy as jay birds, knowing the teacher would come to our house that very day when school was out. What a day this would be. YES! SIREE! We were going to be ready for this special teacher.

The first thing after school that day, mom, Tim, and Monte had to go get winter wood. While they were gone, Beth and I went and set under a magnolia tree, waiting anxiously in the hot muggy weather. The flowers were all bloomed out and cardinals were perched in the tree above us. Nearby, a huge black oak tree rose up with Spanish moss hanging from it as long as Rip Van Winkle's beard.

We looked up at the blue sky and were amazed at the large fluffy, floating clouds which seemed to appear out of no where. Next we decided to pick some yellow buttercups which grew wild around us. Absolutely to our delight, we also found some daisies in which we just had to pick every petal off as we said, "The teacher loves me, she loves me not."

Beth looked up at the sky, and yelled at me to look up at the dark clouds rolling in. A big storm was in the making now. The wind started to blow and the clouds got darker so fast that buckets of rain came pouring down on us in no time. We raced into the house as fast as we could, dripping wet. Quickly, we gathered all our pots and pans to put under all the leaks this old house had. We knew for sure the new outhouse wouldn't leak. There was not enough pots and pans for all the leaks. Even using the old round washtub we took baths in, wasn't enough to catch all the leaks.

New leaks were springing up in the front room. The rain was coming down by the buckets, and the wind, lightning, and thunder were relentless. What if the teacher came now? What were we going to do with all the water in the front room and even on the special chair she was to sit in? Running as fast as she could, Beth grabbed her new shoes (they were already wet) and put them under the old iron cookstove, knowing they wouldn't get any wetter under it.

Mom, Tim, and Monte had not gotten back from getting our winter wood. Beth snuggled up close to me, afraid of the loud claps of thunder and the flashes of lightning. I also wanted someone to snuggle up against, but I was the big sister and had to protect my little sister. It seemed like the storm lasted forever. Finally, the storm ended and out came the sun as if no storm had occurred at all. Only the amazing fresh smell of everything gave it away.

Again we were anxious, only this time hoping Ms. Smith wouldn't come because of all the water in our front room. As fast as we could, we tried to empty all the water out of everything, and we were trying to mop up the front room, when we heard a loud chug! Chug! Chug! And then a clank! Clank! Clank! Hooooly, cow! It couldn't be! No, don't let it be Ms. Smith. Looking out the window, we saw our teacher alone in her old Ford, slowly driving through mud toward our house. We hurried but didn't have time to get all the water out. There was far to much of it on the floor.

As Ms. Smith neared the front door, Beth raced out the back door. Ms. Smith knocked on the door. Knowing I had to open the door for her, I opened it only wide enough for me to slip through, hoping she wouldn't try to come in. Ms. Smith acted like she wanted to come in. I quickly stepped outside. There was no way I wanted her to see all the water on the front room floor. No way I wanted anyone to see how hard we were having it. Yes, we did have a brand new outhouse. Oh yeah, we did!

Ms. Smith asked to see my mom and Beth. I told her mom and my brothers, had gone to get wood. She asked about Beth. I went to the back yard and didn't see her, so I told her Beth must have gone with my mom to get winter wood.

Ms. Smith acted like she wanted to stay for a while. No way did I want her to stay. It would be to embarrassing for our great teacher to see how awful we had to live, even if we did have the best outhouse in this neck of the woods.

Beth sure pulled a disappearing act. Actually it's exactly what I wanted to do more than anything. If only I could hide or something, it was so embarrassing for me. Ms. Smith acted like she wanted to wait for them. I couldn't have that could I? Knowing very well Beth hadn't gone with mom and was hiding somewhere, the teacher simply must not wait for Mom to come back.

Walking up to Ms. Smith, not looking her in the eye, I told her it would be a long time before mom and my brothers would be back because they had to get lots and lots of firewood for the winter. She stood quietly a few moments, then said, "Honey, do they have to work after dark often getting firewood for the family?" Of course, now that I had gone so far with lying, I had to tell her, "Oh, yes, yes! They sure do sometimes." Do you think she believed me? Of course not, but she left to my relief, pretending she believed me. Now how do you like that! This amazing Ms. Smith. Oh, what a teacher!

Her old Ford was hard to start and one of it's headlights was not working. It's wheels spun and she yelled for me to help push the car. It was stuck in the mud. Only weighing about forty pounds, I wasn't much help. She asked me to get a small pan or pot for small pebbles and rocks. Ms. Smith poured the pots full of rocks in front of the back tires. By the time that was taken care of, it was almost dark.

She put her foot on the gas peddle very gently at first, because when her old Ford first started, it choked and sputtered. Finally, to my great relief, she was on her way. She waved good-bye until she was out of sight.

I started to search for Beth, thinking she would be nearby, or maybe hiding some place easy to find. After I'd looked every possible place inside, I went outside and looked up trees and behind bushes, yelling her name as loud as I could, over and over. Then, I went back into the house, thinking maybe I had overlooked something. Again, I shouted her name over and over. I decided I'd search outside one more time before running the mile to our nearest neighbor. I paused a few seconds because I dreaded the thought of running in the dark, even though the moon was shining very brightly. Listening carefully, I thought I heard a cat cry. Wondering what was wrong with the cat, I started toward the sound, but suddenly, I paused, thinking Beth was more important than a cat. I started to leave for the neighbors, but yelled again first. The sound replied but was more like a human cry this time. Rushing as fast as possible toward the cry, it led to the new outhouse.

As I opened the outhouse door, Beth cried, Mommy, mommy, I'm scared. Help me, help me! I told her not to worry, I'd get her out. I told her she would be okay. Mom and the boys will be home any minute now to help me.

Just then, I heard the sound of the boys unhitching the horses. I screamed for them to hurry, that Beth had fallen into one of the outhouse holes.

Both boys came running and mom was right behind them. When they saw the predicament Beth was in, Tim had Monte hold onto his feet while he went down head first to get Beth out. While they were getting Beth out, mom and I went for buckets of water to get Beth washed off as fast as we could. Beth said, "All I wanted to do was to hide from my teacher because I didn't want her to see all the water on the front room floor and my new shoes all wet." Mom said, "Beth honey, the teacher would understand, she is a fantastic teacher."

FLUSHED TOILETS AND TINY KITTENS

Even though the industrial age was going full speed before the 1920's, many people didn't have inside flushing toilets. It was quite a novelty in the beginning. In fact, at that time there were few cars or radios. Looking back seventy or eighty years ago here in America, it is amazing how far we have come today in science and technology.

In the early 1900's it was customary for women, especially during the winter months, to go to another person's house for a quilting bee. A quilting bee was a social event for the ladies of the community and it served as an important means for them to get acquainted. Each lady would bring her own material of wool, cotton, or silk for these fancy quilts they were making. Silk quilts, the fanciest of all quilts, were somewhat like comforters and filled with downy feathers.

We were known to produce the fanciest handiwork in Southern quilts. Peppy Lucy ordered one of these famous quilts from our sector of the country. She bought one with the handiwork of plenum, which means a raised effect. It was to be for her husband, who, at that time, was the President of the United States. The women were so proud to have such an honor.

Lucy was called Peppy Lucy because she didn't allow alcoholic beverages to be served in her large home. These women in quilting bees around the country, were one-hundred percent behind Lucy because many men they knew, or one in which they were married to themselves, had ruined the lives of their families from drinking too much.

Lucy had sent overseas for the silk needed to make this special quilt for her husband. After it was made, one of the ladies had saved a few scraps from this to show the women as a reminder and encouragement to wipe out alcohol.

In 1895 when Grover Cleveland was president, two special quilts were ordered from this little sector of the world. They were to be gifts for a dignitary who was to visit the White House. The White House would furnish all the materials needed to make these honorable quilts. The women were elated. They put all their talents into these quilts and years after the job was completed, they often talked about the tedious work involved.

It was the custom for each family which came together, to supply the materials needed for their own exquisite quilts at the bees. There was always a feast at hand, too, because the women would bring along their favorite food dishes to share and show off at these monthly winter social events. It being an all day affair for all, both women and children present. The quilt frame was usually hooked above on the ceiling of the parlor or front room, where children played under the folds of material which flowed out from it.

Two or three women would set on each side of the quilt with their needles flying, making one stitch at a time. Sometimes they would sing a happy fast song or sometimes they would sing religious songs. Once in a while someone would comment of the current political scene, but the women normally steered away from politics because that was supposed to belong to the mens department. In front of men, women were suppose to be seen and not heard. In some states, if a woman married and had a job teaching, she was expected to quit teaching as long as she was married.

These quilting bees were very important to women because they could talk among themselves about what they really thought about issues. At that time, there was a movement working for a woman's right to vote. Most men were totally against it. Even though their husbands protested, some women wanted to join the women's suffrage movement that was sweeping the country. Of course, this caused a lot of conflict between men and women. At the quilting bees sometimes the conversations would go on about this issue and how to improve things.

The men in the community had their bees, too. Such as barn building, fence making, corn picking, threshing, shocking the small grain, and butchering for winter. The women would usually go with the men to their bees to help a farmer's wife prepare a big feast for the working men. These women would try to outdo each other to make the biggest and best meal possible for these men who worked out in the fields. Everything was made from the freshest and the best. After the work was done, everyone would sing or listen to wild stories which you were suppose to believe, or at least pretend to believe. Regardless of how true they were, they were interesting.

One day three children about three-years-old, were playing under the quilt the women were working on. They were listening carefully to what the women were talking about. They were so interested in what they heard, they stopped playing with some of the empty spools of thread they had. A woman was worried about how to get rid of some day-old kittens, saying, the whole neighborhood was loaded with stray cats no one wanted. Back then there were no animal shelters around. Most owners of cats and dogs fed them table scraps. Otherwise, they had to scrounge in alleys or in peoples backyards, for what little food they could find. Now the time had come where there were so many of them going hungry, something had to be done. No one wanted to see these poor animals go hungry. Of course, for the cats, there were mice and birds, but during the winter months the cats could go hungry, unless you wanted to take food from your own family. The women came up with more than one solution for the lady friend to get rid of her baby kittens. The children were getting very worried about the whole situation.

The family in which the quilting bees took place during that time, was the only family for miles around which had a flushing toilet. Before the bee started in earnest, the owner just had to show it to everyone and demonstrate how it worked. The small children watched in awe as the toilet was flushed. They asked question after question. The lady told them what the flushed toilet was for and how to use it. They were fascinated when she said, If you pooh-pooh, it will be all gone. Of course, right away, each of the children had to go pooh-pooh in a hurry, just to watch it flush.

In the meantime, everyone went back to the parlor to start working again on the eloquent butterfly quilt which they were making. And after thoroughly investigating the new flushing toilet, the children returned and continued to play with empty spools of thread, a tin cup, and an old homemade doll.

The women's needles were flying along stitch after stitch, and they were still talking about what to do with the new batch of kittens. Again the children stopped their playing to listen to what they had to say about the kittens. After a little while the subject was changed. They talked about how they were glad that, as a community they were like family and when one was in need, they all pitched in to help. It was the Golden Rule, as they called it and if anyone didn't follow it in their community, they would confront them about it. The children listened about the Golden Rule, and understood that it meant you should always treat other people like you would want to be treated.

Again the subject turned on what to do with the baby kittens. The children stopped their playing and listened more intently then before, as the women chattered on.

Then the subject got around to the first flushed toilet in the surrounding area. Oh, how wonderful! All the ladies wanted one in their home so they would not have to carry out the bed chamber and empty it in the outhouse when it was cold, stormy, or windy. A bed chamber is a pot with a lid, and it is used in bad weather. It was always the woman's job to empty this pot. So more than anything, all of them longed for a flushing toilet. The children under the quilting frame pretended they were flushing a toilet.

The lady of the house went into the cellar to get some turnips, apples, cabbage, and carrots, for her part in preparing food for the men which would be coming there later from a rally protesting women's rights to vote. All the ladies agreed not to talk about politics, and women's suffrage, when the men were nearby.

When the men gathered in the house to eat, they also were discussing flushing toilets. Only they talked about how there were metal pipes under the house which made it possible for the toilets to be flushed and the contents to go outside.

The baby kittens were all cuddled up on the porch near the flushing toilet bathroom with the mother cat next to them. Once in awhile, one of the ladies would go check on the newborn kittens to uncover them so the mother cat could feed them.

The children decided they all had to go potty again and after hearing so much that day about baby kittens, they gabbed away among themselves on how their mothers did not know what to do with them. They came upon a plan and were sure they could get them all out of this predicament. Looking at each other with happy, pleased, looks on their faces, they knew exactly what to do. Going to the kittens on the porch with the mother cat, one of the children took the mother and the others took the kittens and carried them to the flushing toilet in the bathroom. The mother cat got away and was very upset about the whole situation. She was meowing all over the place. One at a time each of the children dropped a kitten in the flushing toilet, saying, "See we helped our mom. She doesn't have to worry now."

The mother cat was not acting right, the ladies thought. One of the ladies went to check on the new born kittens. Coming back she said, "There is not one baby kitten out on the porch and the mother is wandering all over the place in a dither." Everyone knows sometimes a momma cat will move her babies. The ladies searched every place possible and the kittens were no where to be found. The mother cat was still acting strange.

One of the little boys which had put a kitten in the toilet and flushed it down, tried to tell the ladies how they had helped them out, but none of them could understand him. Then the other two spoke up and told them what they had done. Finally, one lady caught on to what they were saying. When she told the others, they were surprised at what the children had done. Sitting the children down on chairs, it was thus forth explained to them what a flushing toilet was for. With their little hands folded and their heads down, the

21

children just sat there not knowing what to say. Finally a lady said, "What have you got to say for yourselves?"

One of the little boys spoke up and said, "We were going by the Golden Rule to help our moms. Because they kept saying they didn't know what they were going to do with all those little kittens."

OUR THANKSGIVING OPOSSUM

Around the year 1918, in America, there were many people dying from the flu epidemic. In 1929 the stock market crashed, and in the early 1930's, there was a drought.

Many people went hungry and starved. With the pressure of many going hungry, and some dying, my father left my mother with four very young children to raise. He was a musician and wanted to make enough money to pursue his dream to become an inventor like his grandfather, Levi Smith was an uncle to President Hayes.

Levi Smith, my great grandfather, married Fanny Hayes and lived in Massachusetts sometime during the mid-1800's. He invented perhaps, the very first coffee percolator and monkey wrench, but never patented them. His grandson, my father, also had an inventive mind, and was determined to make something of it and patent everything he could. My father made many road trips during his musical profession. The banjo was one of his favorite instruments. He made his own and used cat skins to cover the top of each one of these instruments. People which knew him back then, in the early 1900's, said he could pick the devil right out of the banjo. While he was on one of his road shows in the south, he met and fell in love with a young lady. It wasn't long after this he disappeared. Never to be seen by his wife and children again.

Our fatherless family came close to starving many times during what is known as the Great Depression. It was during this lean period of time, when I was but a child, one experience becomes most vivid:

It all began the first time I saw a opossum with her little babies on her back. She was scurrying along as fast as she could this one late afternoon, a short time before dark. Before I knew it, she disappeared. No one had told me anything about opossums. When I saw this mother opossum, all her babies were hanging on her back for dear life as she hurried as fast as she could with the load of babies. Really they looked big enough to walk by themselves. It seemed so ridiculous to me, I almost had to laugh at the way she was struggling along like she weighed a ton. Of course, at ten years old I hardly knew what a ton was.

There were four children at home and one adult and we were out of all food, except sweet potatoes, and had been eating sweet potatoes and only sweet potatoes for more than two weeks without salt, sugar or any kind of seasoning. There were no jobs or money, Mom was looking desperately to find a farm of some kind to work on, what then was called shares. Finally she found a farmer who needed help and to think he only lived a short mile from us. It's a miracle, we thought. All he could give to harvest on shares was once again, sweet potatoes. His diet for a long time had also, consisted of sweet potatoes, he was a very poor man.

Before the sun came up, Mom and my two sisters were going to the old farmer's sweet potato farm. We had officially ran clean out of food, including sweet potatoes.

Mom wrapped a jug of water in paper, so it would stay cooler. On their way, they stopped by the roadside near a hickory nut tree to gather nuts, with the idea they could eat some for breakfast. These trees grow in abundance in some parts of North Carolina where this story took place. Mom found a rock, it worked good cracking the shell of the hickory nuts. It was important and proper at the time, for women and girls to wear sunbonnets to keep the sun off their faces. Mom and my two sisters laid their bonnets aside on the sweet grass under one of the nut trees.

After cracking some of the hard shells, they were enjoying the rich meats from the nuts, when out of the blue, they were interrupted by snorting noises. Horrified and amazed when they quickly looked up and were looking into the eyes of a long-horned bull. He snorted and pawed the ground in fury and headed straight for them. Needless to say, Mom and my two sisters, took off running as quick as a deer. Trailing behind them were funnels of dust from the bulls hooves. There was no way they were going to risk going back for their bonnets. Mom knew very well they did not have the money to purchase material to make new bonnets. For the rest of the summer of 1932, they had to work without sunbonnets, even while digging sweet potatoes.

Despite the fact that their bonnets were a good long walk from home, getting food was more important. After putting in a full days work, the potatoes were divided. Always the best of the crops went to the farmer. Mom and my sisters were a allotted with two bushels for their share of sweet potatoes.

Everyone was tired, dirty, hungry and sweaty. Each one quickly took a sweet potato to gnaw on.

The farmer kindly offered to hitch up his horses and take them home. It was getting dark on the way home, riding in the wagon, we gazed at the beautiful full moon. The farmer held onto the reins in one hand, while gnawing a sweet potato with the other hand. Flying all around were many fireflies or should I say lightening bugs. The old farmer made up a song about them. He was keeping time with the rhythm of the horses hooves. Each one, was happy just keeping time with the farmers song. The farmer was kind enough to help unload the potatoes when he'd pulled up in front of our house. And he let Mom and the girls know they could come the next day and work for him.

Fall was upon us, and again I was left behind to gather fire wood and clean the yard while mom and my two sisters went to see if they could find some of the wild pecans which grew in our neck of the woods. But before leaving that morning Mom said, "I've seen a opossum around here lately. Most of the time in the early morning, I've seen it going that way." She pointed in the direction. "While we are gone I would like you to try to see if you could kill it and get it ready for our Thanksgiving dinner tomorrow. That is unless of course, you want us all to eat sweet potatoes again."

Lord have mercy, not sweet potatoes again. Oh, no! Wait a minute, sweet potatoes would be better than nothing to eat. You better believe it would be!

Going in the direction Mom had pointed, with all the confidence in the world, I'd find the opossum. Sure I would. At first it seemed like a hilarious funny joke, me not knowing a thing about a creature like that! Except one thing I did know, the mother carried these half-grown babies on her back. To think Mom let me hunt the opossum alone. My, my, my! How grown up I was beginning to feel. Jumping, dancing, and twisting, going around and around, I was thinking how mom trusted me and how grown up I felt at ten-years-old. Being so happy I cut many cart wheels, seeing how long I could stand on my head. After all it would be a few hours before Mom and my two sisters would be home. Man, oh man! It's a wonder I didn't scare the opossum to death with my carrying on, yelling and dancing all around.

Now say you were standing upside down with both hands on the ground looking straight into the eyes of the ugliest big nose, hugest mouthed, hairless-tailed and beady-eyed creature, who was just beside the narrow path and slightly under some brush, with you standing on your head! What would you do? Of course, first thing, step back a little way from it, then squat down. Wait a minute now not, to close and look it over real, real good. Sure you would! If it moved only a tiny bit or the slightest, be ready to run as fast as possible.

This opossum did not move. It was unbelievable, how it just stayed frozen-like right in the spot it laid. I moved closer and stared into it's eyes, and still it did not move, not one little, tiny bit. I don't even think it was breathing, it just laid there very, very still, as if dead. Golly, gee, it's dead I do believe!

I was elated! It made me happier than a June bug to think it was already dead. Yet, I was confused as to how to get my hands on it. I would not want you to know, but I was kinda afraid because I thought it was so very ugly. Since I was not in a hurry, I again stopped and stared it in the eyes. It was so very interesting. I could not help but look at it's big mouth, large teeth, beady-eyes, hairless-tail the ugliest creature you would ever want to see.

I was certain now it was dead. There was not a tiniest move from it. Now I decided to lay down on my stomach for awhile to look it over real good, believing it was dead. It's body, its eyes were like stone. Still not one flinch of it's muscles. I knew it must be dead, but who knows maybe I was wrong and it was sleeping with it's eyes open.

After all, if it woke up it could bite me. So I decided to get a stick to touch it before grabbing it with my hands. All I did was give it one little bitty, tiny push than dropped the stick and ran. I was the one that scared it to death because, after I turned around to look at it, it had not moved from it's position.

How confused can one little girl be? I tried to hold back tears in my eyes but it didn't happen. I put my head in my hands and the tears flowed. My stomach began to hurt because I was getting hungrier by the minute. I had been very careful not to hurt it. Really I didn't hurt it at all and I didn't want to hurt it. In a short time I was thinking about what mom had said just as she was leaving, "REMEMBER, NO OPOSSUM, NO EAT!"

Now I have to forget my heart, head, and stomach which were having a royal battle. My stomach won this one. I wiped my eyes with my sleeves, shut my mouth hard, determined to do what I had to do.

Very slowly and cautiously, I reached for what I thought was a dead opossum and grabbed it's hind legs along with it's long hairless-tail. Happy it had a long hairless-tail, I held it far away from me as quickly as I possibly could. You, betcha I did! To my utter surprise it seemed to stiffen. Holy cow! I do believe it is not dead. Oh my, how awful!

My plans were, if it moved in the slightest, or started to open its large mouth like it was going bite, I would drop it and run for dear life. I was absolutely certain I could out run it, no problem. After all, mom didn't call me legs for nothing! My legs were much longer than this ugly creatures! Oh, yes they were! It was getting a little late and I knew there was no time to waste now. The opossum continued to look dead, though I was beginning to see it as just knowing how to play dead or play, "opossum."

Hanging onto the opossum as tight as I could, I frantically tried to find another stick. Though I did not want it to escape, it was more than I could carry and I dropped it near a log, and scurried around to find a stick. When I returned, the opossum was gone. Ye gads, it can't be gone! We need something besides sweet potatoes for Thanksgiving dinner. Looking around, there it was racing away as lively as you please. Should I be happy or sad? I went in leaps and bounds as fast as I could, there was no way now this opossum was going to get away from me.

Finally, getting in front of it, I thought surely it would head back the way it came from. It did turn when I got to it and I gave it a little push with the stick. Well, guess what? You can believe this or not, this creature fell over and played dead. Oh yes, dead as a door knob! Unreal, stupid and ridiculous, wouldn't you say?

I tried very much to harden my head and heart to the thought of killing it and the idea of it was getting uglier by the minute. Though, it really was ugly to begin with, I wanted to make it even worse. Now, looking at the beady-eyes, bulbous nose, big mouth, scraggly hair, hairless-tailed creature, I was sure it was getting uglier indeed.

Drinking some water for my empty stomach, and to prepare myself for this hard task ahead which I knew I absolutely had to do, I marched ahead toward the opossum.

Only being ten-years-old, I had never killed anything; but my inner sense told me, I better get this over with as soon as possible. One method I used, was to tell myself over and over, others can do it, I can do it! Still I had these awful pangs of feelings inside me that I was not so grown-up after all. So I tried harder to be one and thought about what a grown-up would do in this circumstance? Of course, they would know first of all that you could not eat a live opossum and second of all, that there was no other choice in life but to kill it if you wanted to eat and not go hungry. I only wished this opossum could ugly itself to death or something, and I didn't have to do it.

STOP: AND GO NO FURTHER. IF YOU DON'T WANT THE DETAILS ON THE DEATH OF A OPOSSUM.

I reached for this opossum which played, "possum," with me quiet well. Tightly, I grabbed it's hind legs and hairless-tail and held it as far away as

27

possible, and was ready to run fast if I had too. I had to do this task assigned to me no matter what now. As per suggested by my mom, I brought a hatchet along with me in my hunt for this opossum. Now, I held the hatchet with one hand and the opossum tightly with the other, and I shut my mouth and eyes, HARD. My stomach turned somersaults several times, as I raised the hatchet high in the air to strike it's neck.

Of course, I felt awful sorry about what I had to do to this poor, poor, creature. Even though it was the ugliest thing in the world, I still didn't have the heart I needed to hurt it. Maybe this is why, the hatchet came down and missed the opossum totally. But it scared the opossum out of its wits. That was evident. It gave me such a terrible feeling, so very awful, that I shall never forget it. Now thinking if I open my eyes this time, just a little bit, it would help me to hit the mark. This was almost to much for me, and tears streamed down my cheeks. I pulled myself together and with hatchet in hand, I tried again. This time the hatchet hit it on the side of the neck, and still it played, "possum." This was to much and I laid the opossum down at my feet to cry. While I was boo-booing, this poor ugly creature tried to run away. Now who can blame it? Ye gads, this is horrible! What is a little girl who thought she was so grown-up to do?

I needed to do something before dark and it was coming all to quickly now. In desperation, I thought as the poor, "possum", was struggling to wiggle away. An idea flashed on my brain like a light bulb. I picked up the stick and laid it across it's neck. It struggled so pitifully on the ground I wanted to cry but gulped hard and held it back. Closing my mouth very hard, I placed my feet on both ends of the stick while still trying to hold onto it's hind legs and hairless-tail. With all my strength I could muster out of my fifty-pound body, I yanked on it. It still refused to die. I yanked and yanked to no avail. I was so hungry and tired by now, I wondered how I could continue? But I did. I got my second wind and yanked more. It still did not die, so I had to stop to rest and think on what to do.

After a minutes rest, I had no solution except to keep trying. I yanked again so hard I tumbled over on the ground next to the poor creature. Blood was oozing from it's neck and I felt myself getting sick. I jumped up and bent over holding my stomach as sickness took over. I turned to look at the poor, "possum." It looked very dead now. I needed to be brave and to concentrate on getting rid of the ugly hair on it. Leaving the opossum lay there dead still, I went to get some water and a knife. Common sense told me this was needed and besides that, I often saw how grown-ups used these things in getting an animal ready for eating. The only thing is, I couldn't remember which end the grown-ups started at, when dressing an animal, as they called it. I thought of all this as I ran home and came back with the essential tools needed. I felt helpless when I came back with the essential tools needed and started boo-booing right out loud. But wait a minute, what was that noise I heard? I wiped my eyes and looked around to see the most glorious sight I'd ever seen. My mom and my two sisters were making there way toward me waving and hollering they were home and had come help. Let me tell you, there could never be a happier girl in the world. Now mom could show me how to get the hair off this creature and how to prepare it for dinner.

When mom and the others reached me, mom asked, Why are you crying? As I am sure my eyes were red from tears by now. I shook my head sadly and said, "It's not right mom. It's just not right, to kill even this ugly creature."

Mom told me, many things do not seem right in this world. But you will soon learn you have to do what you have to do to survive in this world. I always will remember these words from my Mom.

That same day, mom showed my sisters and I how to prepare opossum for dinner. She said, We would need to know these things in the real world. Whether it be how to prepare a chicken, a deer, or a opossum. We listened and watched her eagerly as she prepared the meat. And we really did have a feast that day when mom baked the opossum in the old wood cook stove with sweet potatoes all around it. I believe, it was the very best food I had ever eaten.

This particular day, so long ago, taught me great lessons. Besides the knowledge on how to dress almost any animal, I have well learned the lesson of being thankful for the things which we have, whether big or small.

THE HIDDEN CAVE

My mother was a school teacher in the early 1900's. She loved her job of teaching young children immensely and dedicated herself to the cause. But when she married, she knew things would change due to the laws of teaching in schools in America at that time. It was stated as such, "Any woman by which was united in marriage would not be allowed to teach school of any kind but shall devote herself to her husband, children, and home."

She was sad, but this sadness died away as she became a mother to many children. She used her teaching skills wisely with them and read and told stories and taught her children well. She had many stories in which all of us children never tired of hearing. Many times you could see all eight of us gathered around her at night, after the chores were done, to hear these stories. One story in particular sticks true in my mind, even to this day, as she claims it is believed to be true. And so it is the legend of the hidden cave:

Once upon a time, long ago, my mother's uncles and their families left New York to look for a land to settle on in the new territories. Upon arriving at a place we call, North Carolina, they liked it so well they decided to stay and raise their families. Close by this beautiful land, there stretched a gorgeous mountain range called the Appalachians. Today, many people call these mountains, "The Blue Ridge Mountains." Mostly because, on a clear day, they cast a bluish-tint in the skyline above them. This is due to the colors of the trees and the sun's reflection on them.

The parents immediately knew this was the right place to be, because game was plentiful, and the land fertile. And most of all there was plenty of water. Therefore they put together their muscles and built log cabins to live in and planted fields of crops to harvest.

Our relatives lived here happily for a long time. They made friends with the many Cherokee Indians which lived among them and nearby in the Appalachian Mountains. As a matter of fact, these relatives, as children, grew up and played with the Cherokee Indians. They learned much from them including the Iroquois language. Once one of my great uncles, Ted, fell in love and married a lovely Cherokee Indian girl. Her Indian name was, Great Horn, but he called her, "My pudding pie." But it was sad when they were children, because Great Horn was not allowed to attend the, "White mans school." And she had desired to so much. Ted felt sad for her too, when he was a child growing up. It wasn't just Great Horn who could not attend white mans school, but all Indian children were forbidden to go. I tend to believe,

Ted, taught Great Horn many of the things he learned in school. Perhaps, reading and writing.

About this time, many Indian tribes were being forced to move to Oklahoma and live. Some of Great Horn's relatives had already left to go there, Ted and Great Horn, decided it was time for their family to prepare to move also.

Their two oldest children were half- grown boys. The two youngest boys, nine and ten years old, were fast in catching up to their older brothers in strength and size. These boys had learned Spanish from their dad and Iroquois from their mother. In preparation for this long journey, each person had his duties. The boys were to hunt razor-back hogs, deer, and rabbits with their bow and arrows. Then the meat would be salt-dried and put into barrels to take with them. They were not to hunt bears. But they were to gather herbs, fruit to dry, hickory nuts, wild pecans, and chestnuts.

Ted's experience in making the best of covered wagons would come in handy because they would need one very strong to survive a trip which would probably take at least two months. They would stop where needed, to hunt fresh meat and let the animals eat and drink. And do the necessary things to survive. But Ted knew, from his father's stories as well as when he had taken a journey one time himself to Oklahoma and stayed a while, the wagon paths along the way would be very rough. Some passages would worsen by the roughened impressions of earlier wagons' wheels. And yet in other places, the roads, if it rained, would be unpassable. And they would either have to wait it out till it was dryer or find another way. Certain tools would be taken along in case there was a need to fix a wheel rim. And it was likely to occur with the prospects of creeks, rivers and mountains to cross.

Ted's boys knew a lot about surviving in the wilderness, as their father had taught them well from his life among the Indians. They knew, however, there was something special about this journey. In quiet tones, they had over heard their father talk to their mother, Great Horn, saying something about a cave. When they could not stand the suspense one minute longer, they asked their father insistently of what he meant by cave.

He would only say, "You will find out soon enough. In the meantime, you are to be taught more Spanish.

Great Horn had many duties to do before they left in August. There were clay pots, blankets, bags, and moccasins to make, and some extra leather to prepare for the trip. That way, if somewhere along the way they needed more moccasins, they would have the extra material to make them. When she had

31

finished these projects, the last thing she did was to carefully tie the extra leather up with hemp rope.

Now it was almost August and everything was ready to go. Ted asked two of his sons to climb a large black oak tree west of their house and look for four men he was expecting soon. They would be riding in on mustangs. Immediately, the boys did as they were told, and climbed high up into the tree so they could see out across the land. When they had waited for a good two-hours, their father walked over to them and told them it was getting late and they would probably come tomorrow instead. They were to climb the trees and wait as they had today, the same tomorrow.

The next day, just as the boys were getting nice and cozy setting in the large black oak tree which stood on a hill, they could see four prancing mustangs with men on them, riding toward them. Instantly, they both scurried down the trunk and raced toward their Pa shouting and out of breath, "Pa, they're coming this way." Pa nodded in acknowledgment than told them to hurry along and tell Great Horn to prepare food for them. And as they raced away, he hollered after them, and make sure when I bring these men to the house, you take good care of their horses. The boys answered, Yes! As they raced along.

The boys made more hemp rope for the trip, after they had taken care of the mens mustangs. Then, the boys headed down the hill to the little stream in which they had dammed up to make into a swimming hole. They bathed first, than swim, splashing each other and having great fun before they headed home for dinner. They gobbled up all they could eat of the roasted, wild, razor-back hog meat, and beans. And for desert, they ate a few ripe persimmons. An almost ripe persimmon was handed to the youngest of the Spanish men whom were guests. The boys stood by to watch his reaction. When the young man bit into it, his lips started to pucker-up but it didn't seem like he thought it was very funny. Then all the Spanish men, just for fun, started to force one another to taste it, and stood up, and raced after one another.

The next morning, everyone pitched in to get the necessary items loaded onto the wagons. When they were finally ready to go, one giant Spaniard told my father, "Senior, it is time to go." Everything is ready now. Curiously, the boys looked at him and all the other strange Spanish men. Some wore silver breast-plates and silver helmets. They carried strange looking long sticks at their sides in which their father had said these were swords. They had never seen such garb and wondered about these men. What did they want with their father and family? They seemed very friendly and were of no threat to them. But still, these boys were boys through and through, and they were curious of what was going on.

There were two covered wagons full of supplies, and household things, and one wagon was for the members of the family to ride in. Behind one of these three wagons, were two extra horses. Slowly, the wagons fell into a line and headed east. They were only one mile into their trip, when Great Horn told them she had left some of the extra leather behind and needed to go back after it. With so many miles ahead of them, they may have to walk some of it and they would need this extra leather for moccasins.

Instantly, one of their older boys, jumped on the fastest horse they had and away he went to retrieve the leather and bring it back. His hair flew as he rode away at full speed and the horse's mane waved in the wind. After getting to their old house, he found the leather easy enough and pushed it under his arm and with his other hand he held onto the horse's reins. He made the horse go as fast as possible to catch up with them. All of a sudden the horse stopped dead in it's tracks, and he flew off and landed near a timber rattlesnake.

When the little party with the wagons had lumbered on a little longer, Great Horn began to get worried about her oldest son. One of the Spaniard's told her not to worry and he would go to find him. He headed his mustang back towards his friends old homestead. Great Horn turned her eyes toward him as he raced away. His great sword, and silver armor, shimmered in the sunlight while his long dark-hair flew out from under his helmet.

When the Spaniard found the boy, he was fine only his horse had run away and he was walking. He told the Spaniard how his horse had thrown him off close to a rattler. Fortunately, the horse reared up after he fell off, and she came down smashing the snakes head. Indeed the snake had lashed out first and bitten the horse. The Spaniard found the boys horse not to far away fallen and dead. They both rode out together on the Spaniard's mustang, and arrived into the wagon camp, three hours later.

After supper that night, one elderly Spaniard asked everyone to sit around in a circle. He thanked God for their protection and for their good fortunes. First he spoke in Spanish than in broken English. He wanted everyone to listen to what he had to say. From where they were, it would take about two weeks to get to the mighty Mississippi River. There could be no time to waste.

Once they made it to the banks of the Mississippi he gave them permission to take their bows and arrows to quickly find some fresh meat while some of them gathered wood for cooking. Finally, after two days stay on the banks of this mighty Mississippi, a huge barge came and one of the elder Spaniards gave them instructions. He told them in broken English, they would be going up stream about a mile where another barge would be waiting. Then, they would float down stream and land at the right place on the other side.

While at the first stop waiting for the next barge, an elder Spaniard, asked everyone to gather around in a circle and sit on the ground. He said in Spanish, "This is important. There is big trouble in Spanish territory. We must hurry as fast as we can. You and your sons and wife are never to tell anyone about this hidden cave we are going to take you to. No one can find it because it is well hidden behind piles of rocks, dirt and brush. Everyone will start work on clearing this away as soon as we get there. Some of the men will take turns being on watch, while this debris is removed." The younger Spaniard, translated this into English, though all of Ted's family understood and spoke the Spanish tongue well. The elder Spaniard continued on. "Once we break through this debris you will find, a little ways inside, an iron gate. Soon, after we get there, you will see many men come from over the mountain. It will be our men in wagons. There will be about thirty men and ten wagons, along with many mules." After his speech he told them it was time to go.

Three days later, after they had reached the hidden cave and cleared the entrance, twelve Spaniards, some wearing breast armor and helmets, came rushing in. Behind these Spaniards a wagon train was circling around. The mountain was flat on top and the cave was only a few feet from the bottom of the mountain. All the men worked hard for two weeks loading some sort of metal substance. When they finished loading, some went hunting for fresh meat, while yet others, started to conceal the caves entrance. They were in a great hurry it seemed and had not finished the work but left the rest to be done by Ted and his family. Before the four Spaniard friends left, they let Ted and his family know that they needed to cover the ruts of the wagons and any tracks of their horses or mules. It was to appear as if no one had been there.

Thereupon, they also said, "You and your family may live in Spanish territory, and every year about this time, there will be a wagon train to come here where you stand. You and your family are to do the same thing you did for us, as you did this time, and to never tell anyone. In return for this great service, you will be paid well in gold and silver. Now you are welcome in the name of the crown of Spain for as long as you wish to be here and as long as you obey her laws." After embracing each other with tears in their eyes, the four friends and Ted and his family bid each other good-bye. The Spaniards mounted their mustangs and rode away and they all turned to see them ride away into the pink sunset.

It took Ted and his family a couple of weeks to make things look like no one had been there. Not long after they'd finished this task, and they had picked out some land not far from the caves entrance to settle on, their four Spaniard friends showed up. They not only paid them more than they ever dreamed possible but they also stayed long enough to help them build a large log cabin before winter hit. Within the next few years they were able to use this money in the purchase of large amounts of land. Enough to raise cattle and horses, and plant crops of all sorts to harvest. They really did live happily ever after.

FROZEN FACES

I grew up in the deep South where the countryside is charmingly decorated with satiny-sweet curling ferns, whip-poor-wills who whistle and persimmon trees. A place magnolia blossoms grow fat with honeyed-air and the cypress charms you with its dripping moss. A place to call home and to fulfill childish dreams. It is here I became alive for the first time. They say, I howled for the first time when the clock struck midnight. And I grew, just as any child would. One growing experience in my life came when I was at the in between age of fourteen one foot in childhood, the other in adulthood.

It was during this stage of my life, I became tired of being a child. My days were spent daydreaming on being grown-up like my sister, Ivalee. Her dresses were eloquent and visions of her in swirling, flowing clothes marched before my eyes in dreams at night, like tiny dolls.

One summers day, I was sure it was my time to cross over the bridge of being a child and onto the other side of being an adult. The groaning and creaking of this bridge scared me and I was not so sure it was safe but when I lifted my eyes mom walked next to me and guided me until I reached the other side to adulthood. She seemed to know what to do all along. The plop, plop of our shoes beat against the wooden planks and soon I was on the other side. How I see it, this imaginary journey began on this one particular day in the summer, mostly because I wanted it so bad.

Mom had pulled me into her lap that day. With her chocolate-eyes sparkling, and her voice as sugary-sweet as ever, she said, "Beth, how would you like to go up north to see you're sister Ivalee, whom you haven't seen for a while?" I could hardly believe my ears. My inner light was shining like the stars. I slid out of mom's loving arms and stretched my arms like a rubber band round her swan-like neck. I kissed her on the cheek. Oh yes, yes. I should really love to go. Being blissfully happy, I bounced around mom like a playful puppy, squealing with delight and losing sight on trying to act grown-up.

Wow now, slow down child. A smile etched at the corners of mom's mouth. Or I will have to keep you at home and let your sis go instead.

What could I do? I had to calm down because I couldn't let Tara take my place. I sighed heavily, and with regret slowed down as I stood still, and obeyed mom. The only noise I heard was the fervor of my heart beating. It would not calm. My thoughts were scattered wild as wind blown pedals. I imagined the clothes, the elaborate hair-dos and all the make-up Ivalee would be wearing. Except, I pictured myself in her place. And soon I was whirled away in a different world, a world of glamour of my own. I touched my face with powder puffs of different shades of pink. I colored my lashes sleek black to bring out my two pools of pepper-grey eyes. It was invigorating, no, it was soul-ravishing and exciting, and soon it would be real.

Mom rested her thumb and forefinger on the tip of her chin, as if in deep thought. You will be taking a bus out of Charleston and will have to make the trip alone. Do you think you could do that? She brushed away a strand of my red-copper hair, sticky against my cheekbone from the hot moist air. And fixed her gaze on my child-eyes.

I stood stone still, a pearly laughter bubbled out, Of course Mom. I think I am big enough now. I can do it. A second thought raced past and I caught it just in time. "Mom, don't worry I'll be careful." Are you sure?

I bobbed my head up and down like a yo-yo, the thick curls bounced against my neck, and sweat trickled down my back. With one swooping pat to my behind side, Mom said, Okay. Now off with you to bed. It is late. There is a lot we will need to do to get you ready for your trip.

I bobbed my head again and smiled a big grin. Hence, I turned on my heels to go off to bed with my face shiny as satin and giggles bursting forth from my being. I was so excited, it was hard to contain myself. I was positive going to Ivalee's all by myself would be the beginnings of adulthood. I gave Mom a side-ways glance as I turned the corner to run up stairs. I thought, *I must have the greatest Mom in the whole world!*

The next morning came and I was up before anyone else. I had hardly slept a wink all night preparing in my mind what I must do to get ready. I figured I needed to practice, practice and practice some more wearing some high-heel shoes. I ran over to peek in on Mom and she was stirring. She stretched like a long sleek cat than pulled her eyes on me in the doorway. Mmm . . . what are you doing up so early?

I just wanted to get started right away on all the things I needed to do to get ready. Directly, I skipped over to her bedside and hopped in. "Mom, can I ask you something?" "Why sure honey, what is it?"

Can I play dress up with some of you're grown-up clothes, so when I go to Ivalee's I will be able to act like a real grown-up? Oh, yes, also, can I borrow you're high heeled shoes to practice walking in?

Mom brushed her fingers lightly through my hair, as if trying to comb it. An amusing smile spread across her face. "Yes, honey, you can." I jumped out of bed and headed for the closet like a lightning bolt before she had time to finish her sentence. "Thanks mom."

Mom continued, "I have dug out the old carpet bag I made a few years ago. You may use it to put your clothes in. It is setting next to the closet. Mom stretched again. I will help you pack later but first we must do some washing and ironing. And I have some extra material laying around the house, so I thought I would make you and Ivalee matching summer blouses. Would you like that?"

Oh yes. Yes I would. I could feel my face beam bright and full as the moon as I reached for the prettiest dress mom had in the closet and found her black pointed-toe, high-heel shoes. Thus it was, after I grabbed the little carpet bag, I had everything needed, and dashed into my room.

So it was, I dressed-up, swirling this way and that way, observing myself in the long narrow mirror. That was the easy part, the difficulty came when I tried to practice to walk in the high-heel shoes. I practiced and practiced but always seemed to wobble around and sway as unsteady as a dancing bear. Unnoticed to me, all this time, mom had been standing in the doorway and when I made my last attempt to walk straight, I must of looked rather ridiculous, sliding here and there on the wooden floor. Mom in the meantime had come in to sit down on my bed and watched me with amusing eyes aglow.

All it took was one short side-glance at mom and I lost it. I tittered and went tumbling down onto the hardwood floor. Mom convulsed into laughter by now, holding both sides with her hands and falling over on the bed. I laughed too, till my eyes were watery and my sides hurt.

Three days later the first moment the sun peeked over the hills, I bounded out of bed to push open the window and inhale the sweet fresh summer air. Scents from the magnolia, which was planted close by my window, drifted in and filled the air like heavenly daze. All the washing and ironing had been done and today was the day to do the packing. It was hard not to act child-like to the core and do somersaults and cartwheels right there. But somehow, I kept from it.

Mom helped me stuff the last of the clothes into the bag including the two matching summer blouses she had just finished sewing for Ivalee and I. We had pushed and crammed every garment piece possible into it. We even managed to wedge some make-up which mom had given to me, in the corners. By then, the poor little valise looked pretty pitiful. It was coming apart on all sides at the seams. Mom hightailed it out to the shed and came back to fix the problem, towing a hemp rope in her hand. I stood there perfectly still while mom tied the rope around the canvas-bag to hold it together. The bag was ugly and its appearance embarrassed me to no end. Somehow, I bit my tongue and did not express my views about it to Mom. Truth to say, I was glad I did. Mom rubbed her hands together as if getting dirt off them. Well, I think that will hold till you get to Ivalee's. She will help you, I am sure, to tie it up again when you are ready to come back home. Now She looked at me for a second then continued. How about breakfast?

Soon with bellies full, mom and I strolled down the dusty lane and headed west toward town. Sometimes, I skipped ahead of her and, sometimes, I'd slow down and walk beside her. We skirted the little foot bridge where a whimpering creek, hollowed down from the mild winter and dry summer, choked its way beneath and beyond, following a line of cypress trees.

It wasn't long and we arrived in the small town of 1500 people and, it always seemed an oddity to say, 2,000 animals. The towns people were friendly and weren't shy to boast of it. Good-day to you, Mrs. Gareth. A thread-like man tipped his little red cap which he always wore precariously slanted on his head. His bald head flashed shiny as an egg in the bright sun. This would be Mr. Finley. He owns the barber shop.

Good-day to you too, Mr. Finley. Mom nodded her head graciously and plastered a smile across it.

"Lovely day, isn't it?" Said a plump as a dumpling lady with rosy cheeks, as she passed us by. This is Mrs. Applebee. "She will be teaching algebra this year in my school. I sure hope I don't have her. I heard she stings your fingers with a ruler over the pettiest things. I pulled my head round to take a better look at her as she sauntered by. She was wearing her hair in a neat little bun at the nap of her neck. The kind I liked and the kind I had attempted at before the mirror this morning. I patted my thick bun positioned in the same angle as hers, but somehow it wasn't as neatly formed, and strands of hair untidily stuck out of it. And I am embarrassed to say, it took me two long hours to make it presentable. *I wonder,* I thought as I touched my index-finger to my chin, just like mom does, *If there is a certain trick to fixing buns right.*

"Well, here we are!" Mom said as she plopped the canvas bag down by her feet. "Wait right here. I'll be right back with the tickets."

I nodded in reply and set down in a chair close by, dragging the ugly bag with me. It was hard to sit still. I wanted to do child-like things. Like jump up and down, and run around, whooping it up and holler. It was hard to be a lady. I tried to convince myself, *It would be good practice.* And told myself that over and over while waiting for mom. Finally, mom returned with a slender piece of paper. She handed it to me. Now you be careful and don't loose these. She chatted on, as I noticed the nice big bus pull into the depot. It's steel shell shimmered in the sunlight. And for heaven sakes watch what you are doing and don't go day-dreaming and miss you're place to get off the bus. Mom eyed the bus and looked back at me. I thought she might cry, Well, I guess this is it. She embraced me tightly and kissed my cheek. Now you be good, you hear and don't forget to call me when you get to Ivalee's.

I will Mom . . . I will call you and please don't worry about me.

With valise in tow, I headed toward the bus. Half-way there, I pulled around and blew Mom a kiss.

Tears were falling down her cheeks. I didn't know growing up was sad.

It was six hours before we came to a little town in which the bus would stop for an hour lay-over. Here I would catch another bus which in turn would take me to the end of my journey. I was glad for this change because the last hour on the road had been so bumpy, I thought my teeth would chatter right out of my head. Immediately, I went to the ladies room, as city folk call it.

The thought occurred to me, *how strange it feels to be in such a luxurious ladies room, when at home in our backyard, all we had was an old outhouse and you certainly couldn't freshen up there.* But I was a city girl now, and I tilted my chin upward just a little bit as I fumbled with my bun to put some loose hairs back into it. Next, I decided to change into the new blouse Mom had made me.

After changing, I checked the mirror to see if all was in order. *Just a couple more touches*, I thought. I dabbed some sweet-smelling cologne behind my ears. Then, I put on my favorite pale-pink lipstick, smacked my lips together like real grown-ups do, and smugly grabbed my things and walked out. I made a bee-line to the area in which I would be boarding the next bus. There were not many people waiting there, yet.

There was one elderly man seated on a bench with his bulbous nose stuck deep into a newspaper. Next to him stood a lady as lean as a rake, with harsh features, awkwardly standing there with her arms crossed. Obviously angry about something. A few stragglers happened by. And across from me was a bum sprawled out on another one of the wooden benches with a newspaper over his face. I hoped he was not going on the bus too. I had heard about city bums which were winos.

People looked up from what they were doing to see me, a girl in a low-cut chiffon blouse who carried a rather ugly piece of luggage. They did not smile and I could feel cold eyes which seemed to look clean through me. I was exceedingly embarrassed and could feel a vibrant rush of blood come to my cheeks. My eyes diverted from their cruel looks and swept the area. I found a safe place to stand and dropped the ugly bag at my feet.

Soon the roar of the bus's engine drowned the air and the next thing you knew, it pulled up to the curbside. I pulled my eyes toward the door as it swung open and let people out who frantically pushed and shoved at each other to get down the stairs. It seemed crazy to me at how rude they were to each other. My mind began to wonder as I waited for these rude people to leave. I thought about Ivalee and what she would be like. After all, it had been over two years since we'd seen each other. She wrote to us a few times and spoke often of how it took her a while to get use to the big city life. As a matter fact, she let us know in her last letter, how city life had grown on her now and she rather enjoyed it.

I noticed by now, crowds of people were standing around waiting just like me to board the bus. Right then, I felt lonely and scared, and wondered if I could ever get use to the city life as Ivalee did. I scanned the scene around me and thought, *no one is even smiling and they carry the longest drawn-down faces I've ever seen.* No sooner were these thoughts out of my head, than out of the corner of my eye, I saw a red cardinal flutter over my head and land on a nearby bush. I heard the hum of bees close by and saw that they were in a patch of flowers planted nearby. Unannounced, and right before my eyes, a couple of the bees made a headlong dive at me. One landed near my ear and I shook my head and, luckily, it flew away and did not sting me. Another one landed on my neck and I quickly lowered my head as if I were getting ready to stand upside down.

Lucky again, it flew away. Still I was afraid another one would find me and I stood there petrified as wood, afraid to breathe or move a muscle. Soon, however, a couple more bees were at my head buzzing around and it was getting to be a rather maddening thing.

I didn't know what to do. It seemed it didn't do any good for me to move to a different position, they just followed me there. About the time I was pondering my dilemma, I felt it. A horrible sensation of something crawling on the sweaty skin of my back. And the first thing which flashed through my

41

mind, was it was a horrible poisonous spider? I don't know what made me think of that, but I knew it was silly to think such a thing with bees buzzing all around me. It had to be a bee!

I didn't have much time to think on these lines because the next second a sting tore into my flesh right under where my bra fastened. I let out a blood curdling scream. I knew I wasn't acting like a lady, but I couldn't help it. Mostly, I didn't care at that point. I pulled my eyes around to some of the people standing there like marble. None moved to help nor offered any kind of support. I was confused and didn't understand it. In my little part of the world, where I live, people go by the Golden Rule. Someone would have rushed to my side in an instant.

Yet another sting dug in me, and by than I was flinging around like a puppet on a string. My eyes felt watery and they winced from the pain. My cheeks were flushed and I felt sweat trickle down my armpits. I called out in misery for help. But no one came.

It seemed as if, every place I looked peoples eyes stared, unfriendly and cold out of frozen faces. *Lord have mercy.* I thought, *is this how city folks act?* It is true, a crowd of city folk gathered around me in a circle, as if they were watching some freak side-show. I was frantic by now. I didn't want to yank my blouse off in front of everybody and it took all of which was in me not too. I certainly couldn't run to the ladies room, either, and risk the chance of missing the bus

It seems out of the blue and as if by magic, there appeared in the crowd a rickety old lady which elbowed her way toward me. This strange woman was a relief to me even if she did have an odd appearance. She uttered cooing words to me as she came closer and touched me on the arm with her gnarled fingers. Surprised, I jumped. After a time though, the words she spoke had an salve like affect on me. Her bony hand patted my arm and I felt better. At least until I felt the next sting rip away at my skin. I thrashed my arms around and almost knocked the poor old lady down.

In the meanwhile, the lady had managed to shuffle behind me and I felt her hot breathe on my neck as she spoke. Now honey, I am going to lift up you're blouse and undo this cumbersome bra strap. So just you stand still for a minute. With cold fingers she managed to undo the bra strap. And with one swoop of her hand she had shooed a bee away. I settled down quickly after that and realized this little old lady almost looked like a fairy. She even acted like one, to me. With silvery-white hair and an undescribable twinkle in her eye and rosy-cheeks which settled well with the rest of her plump body.

Next thing I knew, she reached into her purse and drew out a tube of ointment which she immediately opened, and applied the salve-like ointment on the two stings I'd just incurred. She fastened my bra swiftly and drew down the blouse. Quickly, she handed me the tube and smiled a toothless grin saying, "you use this and soon you'll be as good as new."

I glanced at the tube in my hand than looked up to say thank-you and discovered the little old jovial lady was gone. The people around me who never made a move to help me, were in a line and loading on the bus. I quickly grabbed my old bag and lined up too. I was beginning to wonder about this great city-life so many spoke of. Except for the one fairy-like lady that came to my rescue, there was no one else I could say was very nice. Maybe being grown-up is not as great as I imagined.

My turn to board the bus came swiftly and I took my turn graciously. Until that is I stepped up onto the second step. To my utter amazement I fell up the step. Of all the things in the world, I fell up not down. I straightened myself and tried again but I fell stumbled and fell again. How totally ridiculous I felt.

When I looked up the bus driver had a twinkle in his eye. One kind of like the little old lady who had just helped me. He said, "Are you okay?"

He actually wanted to know if I was okay. Maybe he would be number-two city person to be found to be nice on this trip. I thought.

I sniffled, Only my feelings are hurt.

Once on the bus it resumed to the atmosphere, the same cruelty of faces and people. I could tell the minute I turned my head around to see them. Their sour faces reminded me of one time when my friend took a big bite out of a green persimmon. Boy, did her mouth twist and pucker-up into such a sour look and it was stuck frozen like that on her face, for quiet awhile. Of course, not stuck as long as it seemed these city-folks kept theirs. It seemed hilarious to me, to see how funny looking these city peoples faces really were. And it seemed to be harder and harder, as we rumbled along, to control that laughter bubbling in me. All I wanted to do was to jump in a hole and pull a cover over me, so I could have a real good laugh. I decided to twist my face into every shape possible to keep from laughing out loud. I managed to come up with a real ugly frown.

I reconsidered this idea because I figured it would make my face look soured and frozen just like theirs. And besides, how in the world could I keep twisting my face in shapes and still act like a grown-up lady? After pondering this question, I realized I really wasn't as grown-up as I thought I was. Come to think of it, I began to realize it was so much more fun to stay plain old fourteen, for just a while longer. It felt mighty good to be a kid again.

PART TWO

YEARS 1936-1949

THE TIGHT BLACK CREPE DRESS

The purpose of this short true story is not so much the near death experience as to let you picture how modest some of North American society was in the 1940's.

It was one of the most embarrassing times of my life. Though in today's society it may not be embarrassing to some people to wear a dress a few inches above the knee, it definitely was considered a NO! NO! in the 1940's. And if someone would have worn a bathing suit like they do now in the year of 2000, it would have been a real shocker. You could have been picked up for indecent exposure.

My friend Anne and I had been good friends all through school, and in 1940 we were lucky enough to get a job at the same place at a raw asbestos rock plant in Charlotte, North Carolina. Our job was to tend a slabber machine which shredded the asbestos rock into very light weight fibers. We were there for one year when Pearl Harbor was attacked and war broke out. The asbestos plant was running full speed after the war broke out and there was no way we could get time off to go shopping. In fact, if you came to work two minutes late, you could get fired. There were others eager to take your place.

One day Anne said, "Hey Fanny, let's go north where the pay is better." As I was supporting my two sisters and my mom, it was necessary to try to make more money. In those days there was very little welfare to help you. We really had no idea where to go. But after discussing it a few days, we decided to go to Baltimore, Maryland to try our luck.

There was so much work to do before we left. Neither of us had decent clothes for the trip and to look for work. One day after work, we rushed to the nearest store to buy material to make ourselves nice dresses. After running the mile to the store, we were so out of breath, it was hard to tell the clerk what we were looking for. The clerk took us to the back of the store to the material. We stood there in total amazement looking at all the gorgeous material. There was so much of it, and everything was so beautiful, it was almost impossible to pick out anything. Because neither of us had much money, we had to buy as little as possible for our dresses. Finally I picked some gorgeous black crepe material. The clerk said it would be two dollars and twenty cents. I only had two dollars. Anne loaned me the twenty cents. I was worried about not having enough material to make a dress.

48

The next few days we were as busy as could be cutting out our material. I was short of material, and I made my dress tight and a little shorter than they were wearing back then. I remember thinking to myself that this dress was real sexy. OH! YEAH! Putting it on after it was finished was a chore. I had to double sew the seams to keep them from busting open. To top it off, this dress was three inches shorter than anyone else was wearing. I wondered if it would look too brazen to search for work in. I had chosen black to look older and more sophisticated, but how can you look sexy and sophisticated at the same time? Anyway Anne approved of my dress. I knew she would.

Some of our friends last name was Smith, and to tease them we said we were going to Baltimore to get away from so many Smiths.

Arriving at the train station and asking for tickets to Baltimore, the ticket agent said, Baltimore. He explained in the North it is called Baltimore with a short "ti".

It was our first time away from home. We could hardly contain ourselves, we were full of excitement. There was little money left after buying our tickets and we had to save enough to pay for a place to sleep. Realizing it might be a few days before we found work, we boiled three dozen eggs, hoping they would last us for three days. We absolutely could not spend the little money we had on anything unnecessary. While on the train we would go to the bathroom, eat one egg at a time to make them last, then we'd wrap the shell in toilet tissue and place it in the trash.

At last we arrived in Baltimore early one morning. The very first thing we saw when the train stopped was a huge sign saying, SMITH'S MANUFACTURING CO. This caused us to giggle, almost uncontrollably for a while. Teasingly we talked about heading back south to get away from all the Smith's that were being manufactured here.

After getting off the train in Baltimore, we hailed a cab to take us to the address we were going to. Instead of the cab driver taking us straight to the address we gave him, he drove us around many, many blocks out of the way. Since we were green horns at the time, we didn't know the address we wanted was only three blocks from the train station. To late I realized the cab driver's plan was to make more money. It was a well learned lesson for us.

After we had a few pay days, we eagerly made plans to go by street car to see Chesapeake Bay. We dressed to look our best, and, of course, I wore my tight, short black crepe dress. BOY! OH! BOY! Would I look sexy.

Getting to Chesapeake Bay early on this gorgeous, hot day, not a cloud in the sky, we decided to rent a rowboat and try rowing to the lighthouse. It was a long way across the bay. So what! We had all day. There weren't many people out this early in the morning, so we had our choice of rowboats. As if that made a difference, because we didn't know a thing about any kind of boat. We had never been near lakes or the ocean. We thought the smallest boat would be the best to try to row. Big, big mistake!

We had brought lunch for a picnic and plenty of water in half gallon canning jars. Obviously we were out for fun, and thought we had plenty of time. We splashed in the water and enjoyed watching the birds dive for fish. Before we knew it, it was noon. We'd better get started, we thought, if we wanted to get to the lighthouse. Neither one of us had ever rowed a boat, and at first it was really hard to row in unison. Finally we got the rhythm of it. Leisurely we rowed and rowed, laughing at anything and everything. To us even the birds diving for fish was funny.

Looking up at the sky, to our amazement we saw dark clouds rolling in from the west. The wind had started to blow, and we were about halfway to the lighthouse. But no little wind, or should I say strong wind, was going to stop us from reaching the lighthouse! No way. Not us. We were still determined to reach it. The wind started blowing harder, the waves grew higher, lightning cracked, and the clouds got darker. Suddenly, the clouds burst with a huge down pouring of rain along with more relentless thunder and lightning. The rain came down like something was pouring buckets of water on our heads.

We were scared out of our wits. The rowboat was tipping out of control, with water coming over the sides, regardless of how fast we dipped it out with our two half gallon canning jars. All the fun was quickly sapped out of us. Anne was thrown part way out of the boat. I hooked my feet under the seat and reached for her, almost tipping the boat over. The waves threw us, first one way, then another. We worked feverishly to bail out water with both jars. We were helpless, tossed around violently in the rain, wind, and thunder. It was like a living nightmare. We screamed at the top of our voices, knowing no one could hear us. Though absolutely certain this was the end for us, there was no way we'd give up. We continued to bail as fast as we could and to struggle to keep the boat upright, despite the fact that it was tipping dangerously. We knew we could be dumped into the water at any moment.

Lightning was flashing more and more frequently, with thunder cracking right behind it. I prayed to God not to let us drown out there, not to let it be our time. Then in the distance, when the sky was lighted from flashes of lightning, I saw a large vessel of some kind. We screamed and yelled as loud as we could. Standing up and waving was not possible because the boat was rocking too violently. We were completely exhausted and almost ready to give up, when suddenly a fog horn sounded faintly. I yelled at Anne to stop dipping water for a minute. She screamed back, "The boat will sink with one more strong wave and we will be gone!" I screamed, "Anne! Listen, it's the sound of a fog horn!" Then the fog horn sounded closer with shorter intervals. Amidst the lightning flashes, a large tugboat not far away emerged from the gloom.

At that moment a huge wave selected to hit us broadside, tipping our little rowboat over. We clung to the side of our overturned boat for dear life, while one man in the tugboat yelled at us, as he went down the ladder and into the water with three life jackets on one shoulder, which had a long rope tied to them. Another man tried to throw a life ring to us, but we were too far away. We were bouncing around hanging onto our little boat. Just as the first man reached us, another man plunged in and swam toward us. It seemed like an eternity before he reached us. One man grabbed Anne because she was gasping, and the other grabbed me and helped me to put on a life jacket. With the next big wave, he lost his grip on me and I went under. As I came up he grabbed my hair and pulled me closer to him. The tugboat itself was rocking violently as we approached. A man on board tied a rope under my arms, and pulled me up to the railing, then helped me slide into the boat.

Up until this point I hadn't given my tight black crepe dress a thought. About all I was thinking about was saving my life. Now with these four men standing over both of us, actually staring because my dress was very short and tight (my garter belt holding up my stockings looked ridiculous) the knowledge of my apparel suddenly came rushing back to me. Surely this was better than any movie back then. Have you ever been relieved, thankful, and very, very embarrassed at the same time? This combination is unreal. Quickly someone went to get blankets to cover us up, but first they had to give us a tongue lashing to last a life time. They took turns telling us how we had almost lost our lives and how foolish we had been. While sitting there with my eyes and mouth closed, and my legs crossed, I wondered how in the world I was going to get off the tugboat with this horribly short, tight black crepe dress on. I had wanted to look sexy, but this was ridiculous.

The storm had let up some. The lightning had moved farther away with thunder rumbling now and then. I dreaded the thought of getting off the tugboat when we arrived at the dock. We sat silently with our heads down about as far as we could hold them, hoping there would be no more tongue lashing. The men were really too busy controlling the tug to think about what had happened.

I couldn't stop thinking about how I was going to get off the tugboat. Can you imagine how I looked with this tight black crepe dress up to my butt, with a garter belt holding up my stockings, bare footed, and as wet as a drowned rat, sitting on the violently rocking tugboat. One of the men gave us hot chocolate to drink or spill.

Guess what! They forgot about the blanket for our laps. I do believe they did it on purpose, just to look at our legs. We sat there blushing, not knowing what to do with these four men staring at us. Yes, the weather had been hot and it felt good to be soaking wet.

A big fight broke out among two of the men. It was hard for them to fight with the tugboat rocking back and forth, even though by now the rain had slowed down. The thunder had completely stopped, but the waves were still high. It was outrageous for these men to be on the deck pounding each other. Suddenly the captain yelled. He needed help at the stern. Both men raced to help the captain.

Anne and I couldn't look up at them. We were too embarrassed. All I wanted to do was to fall over and play dead. Nobody told me that crepe material would shrink, and now it was clear up to my butt. Yep! I sure did want to look sexy, but not this sexy!

When we got to the dock I didn't know whether to hide somewhere on the tugboat, run as fast as I could down the pier, or simply jump into the bay and swim out of sight. Just imagine this almost full bloomed, young skinny girl running down the street with a tight, very, very short black crepe dress, running for dear life, her breasts bouncing and her dress so short you could see her underpants. That's not all; her garter belt holding her silk hose up surely would be a sight for sore eyes. OH! YEAH! There was no way I was going to put on a show for anyone like that.

Fortunately, a gentleman brought us a blanket as they were docking the tug. It was too big for my small size, so he went back to find a smaller one, and he helped me tie it on around my waist. Not looking at him, I said, "Thanks, sir." I didn't want to talk to anyone, but he seemed to want to talk. He said, "Now listen, young lady, if I was in this kind of predicament wouldn't you do the same for me?" As I sat there with my head down and my legs crossed, I said, "Yes sir" very shyly. He then turned to talk to the captain.

While I sat on the bench, I wondered how I could ever get on a street car on a Sunday evening, the bus crowded, my hair a mess, barefooted, and of all things, a blanket tied around my waist. Move over fish, here I come, I thought. Suddenly there was a tap on my shoulder. The man who had given me a blanket said, "You two young ladies wait for me at the end of the pier and I will take you home." Listen to that! He actually called us ladies. Before we were called girl or kid. Sure made me feel more grown up. He was the nicest person you would ever want to meet, and he was kind enough to remind us that young girls have to be careful as some people would take advantage of beautiful girls like us. We never saw this man again, but he left an impression on us to this very day. Anne and I were so very grateful God saw fit to let us live to see another day.

The gentleman let us out at the curb. Quickly I said, "Here's your blanket. Thank you so much!" I was in a hurry to run down the sidewalk, because two neighbors were in their yards. I whizzed by them like a flash of lightning, hoping by flying by them fast enough, they wouldn't see me.

Anne took her time getting out of the car and the neighbors said, "What's her hurry, Anne?" Anne said. "She has some urgent business, you know what I mean." Guess I'll never know if they saw me in my ridiculous, very short and tight black crepe dress. One thing is for sure. I will never, ever wear another black crepe dress.

HOPPING JOHNS

When I was a teenager, I felt my mom's cooking was the very best in the whole world. So why should I learn to cook? After all, there was no way I could compete with her. Little did I know how much things would change as I grew older.

After I married, I wished I had paid more attention to how my mom cooked. She had tried to teach me, there was no question about that. Me, being as stubborn as I was, had a mind of my own and I certainly did not think cooking was that important then. There were too many other interesting things to do than learn to cook. Yak!

The first few days after I married, I had a rude awakening. My cooking was lousy. Worse yet, I dreaded my husband finding out what a lousy cook he'd married. The second night of marriage came, and I was determined to prepare a fancy meal. I was desperate and wished there was some kind of crash course I could take before I attempted this chef's approach of preparing a meal. A big meal! I went to the store twice because I didn't write down all the items I needed on a grocery list. I hadn't even thought of that idea yet. I cleaned everything spotless in the whole house. Everything looked perfect for this elegant dinner I had planned.

Finally I prepared the meal. It looked delicious and I just needed a few finishing touches. I had to hurry because my husband would be home at any second. I quickly dusted the potatoes with salt so I could mash them, the salt lid came off and half the shaker of salt dumped into the potatoes. I was mortified. What was I going to do? I grabbed a spoon that was in the sink and skimmed off the tops of the potatoes the best I could than proceeded in mashing them as directed in the, "How to Cook," cookbook I had just purchased at the store.

Next came the gravy, as per directed in the cookbook. Somehow, it didn't look quite right. It didn't have the smooth consistency in which my mother's always had, so I decided to add a little extra cold water to cool it down, and beat it up nice and smooth. What a disaster that was. Besides having this brown sauce all over the front of me, it also had ended up somehow, all over the kitchen wall in front of me and all over the kitchen counter. As if that was not enough, what was left of the brown gravy which was suppose to be thick and smooth, was now thin as water except for the lumpy parts, which were many.

Luckily, the salad didn't look to bad even though I wasn't sure if I was suppose to cut up the core that came on the bottom part of the lettuce. The cookbook didn't tell me either way, so I opt to keep it, because, I figured it would give it a nice crunch. I cut it up in little tiny chunks. Also I sliced big fat juicy tomatoes and lined the salad bowl with them. At least there was some hope, everything looked good in the salad bowl. I wasn't long into praising my work till I smelt something funny. And turned just in time to see smoke rolling out of my oven. *Oh, no.* I thought. *My cake!* It was burnt as could be on top, so I started to scrape the burnt part off on top, though, because it was so hot, it was hard to hold, even with the pot holders. By now, I wanted to sit down and cry. But I didn't have time too, because my husband would be home any minute. I thought, *Maybe he won't notice how terrible the food looks. After all he is a man and I've heard it said before, "Men usually don't notice the same things women do."* I glanced over at the shriveled up roast beef which numbered in the same sequence as the poor burnt chocolate cake I'd attempted. Burnt crisp and black as night.

I felt a lump in my throat rise, as I was setting the table, but managed to swallow hard to subdue the fears. I used my best silverware which was two little spoons and one knife which we would have to share to cut up the roast beef. I had a set of four china plates which shone bright and new as I set them on the little table. They were a wedding present from one of the relatives and I was very proud of their dainty little flowers which flounced the edges. Next, I set the tiny glasses, also a wedding present, on the table and filled them with red wine. *A little extra added touch,* I thought. Last but least, I set the prepared food on the table, such as it was. The next moment I looked up and my cheerful husband walked through the door. I smiled through my teeth thinking, *I hope he remains this cheerful after he tastes my food.*

When my husband and I set down before this feast, my husband took one quick bite, then he took another. I watched him eagerly, to see his reaction. What I expected and what I got are two different things. I expected a real sweet smile and, I was even geared up to hear him tell me how wonderful the meal was and, how gorgeous I looked.

Instead, he gave me a weak smile just as he gulped hard and reached for the glass of wine before him. In turn, I took a bite to see why he had a hard time swallowing the mashed potatoes. I almost gagged and spit it out before I could manage to grab the glass in front of me fast enough to drink down some liquid. Not only were the potatoes still too salty, they also tasted like soap. I had forgotten that I laid the spoon I'd grabbed out of the sink, in some dish soap I had spilt earlier. Well, so much for my elegant meal that night. My husband really didn't complain about it. And I was thankful he was understanding. So much for me trying to masquerade around the idea that I could fool him into thinking I could cook.

I can say my next attempt at preparing a meal, happened with a little improvement to the skill. I didn't burn anything to the crisp, at least. However, I did leave the gall bladder inside the chicken I cooked, which had the same effect as eating a piece of bitter wormwood root. Still, however, I had the same problem with the old salt shaker my great grandmother gave to me out of her treasured things, the lid came right off. It only dumped a fourth of its contents instead of half this time around. With that particular meal, I had attempted my first pie crust and filling. It was to be a lemon meringue pie. I still to this day do not know exactly what went wrong. I have my suspicions that the oven temperature was set to low, because I seemed to have cooked the thing forever. It looked fine on the outside, it wasn't even burnt. However, when we attempted to bite into it, the pie crust was as hard as a rock.

At that meal, my husband and I both were a little reluctant to bite into anything. Especially, after the roast beef dinner experience as of a couple nights before. So we took tiny little bites, with hands resting nonchalantly on our drinks, just in case. Our faces had half-smiles on them, pretending like everything was alright. We didn't get far into eating much of the dinner that night. I was so embarrassed. But my husband quietly turned his head toward me and said, "You'll do better next time." We went out to eat that night. Nonetheless, I promised myself the next dinner I made would be the most delicious ever. Moreover, I will dress so sexy on that night, it will knock his eyes out.

My most embarrassing moments I ever had, in the cooking experience, was still right around the corner and I didn't realize it. It all began one day when my husband came home from work as cheerful as ever, and bounced into the kitchen and said, "Honey, are hopping johns hard to make?" I said, trying not to appear totally ignorant, "My goodness, of course they will be easy to make."

His eyes were steady upon me as he said, "Can you make some for our dinner one night soon?" I nodded my head. Are you sure you want to try to make them?

I crossed my fingers behind my back, as I said, "It will be very easy. I have seen my mother make them before."

We lived upstairs in this older home and another family with two children lived in the basement. The day after my husband asked me if I could make hopping johns, the lady who lived in the basement, Mrs. Bent, came to visit me. Since I had taken care of her two children several times, she wanted to ask me to come to a "Big Feed" they were going to have. She told me it was very special and she could not tell me what it was for. My husband and I agreed to go to it with the idea I would bring a nice big pot of hopping johns. When I was a kid, I remembered how I use to watch mom make hopping johns dishes with fat back and rice. Somehow, I figured I could do the same. I was so proud of myself when I could act like I knew what I was doing when I talked to Mrs. Bent about bringing this pot of hopping johns to her party. She told me right off, I didn't need to do this, but I insisted on it until she agreed to it.

The next couple of hours, I was very curious at what this big surprise could be but I kept my mind busy with other things to forget about it. For one thing, I needed to go right away and buy the necessary things to make this hopping john's dish. Once supplied, I can get busy and make it, for the next day was the big shindig. Or "Big Feed," as she called it. I scanned through the new cookbook I had and there was nothing in it at all about hoping johns. Then the thought occurred to me to call on my grandma. Since she lived not far from me it would not be a long distance call. Besides, she taught my mom how to cook.

After a couple of sessions on the phone with grandma, I finally arrived at the place where I thought I knew what to do to prepare this dish. The only thing that was amiss was something to do about the part she called, "Fat back." I still didn't quite understand what fat back was, and every time I would ask grandma, she would go off into this spill which lasted two hours, about how they raised their pigs back in Minnesota. She did say though, "Hopping johns are beans or black-eyed-peas. You usually make them with a hunk of fatback. Its real good if you spread it over rice." Wow, that sounded so simple, I just knew I could do it.

The next day, I still didn't know what fat back was except pigs had something to do with it. Likewise I called grandma again to find out, and this time she didn't go into the spill about their raising fat old hogs, but instead told me straight out it was the back off a hog. As I hung up, I realized, if I could find the fat off the back of a hog she is talking about, which you find in the grocery stores, this would be a piece of cake. Hopefully not the kind of cake I make!

Now I could show my husband what a good cook I was becoming. I sat down on our couch to think the details over. I turned my head this way and that, while I figured things out. *Of course, it would make sense to cook the black-eyed peas a little longer than the rice, since the beans were bigger in size. This would also mean, they should have more water on them*, I thought. *The rice on the other hand, since they are much smaller in size, would not need to be cooked very long and would need very little water.* Presently, with everything straight in my mind, I was ready to go full speed ahead. Straightaway, I hurried off to the store to buy the supplies needed. After all, the big shindig was tomorrow.

The following morning, I washed the black-eyed peas just as grandma had mentioned to do. After this, I found a big kettle in which I placed them in to be cooked and filled the kettle up with plenty of water. I threw in the fatback and turned the burner on full blast, careful to keep an eye on the contents so it wouldn't overflow. Later, as I glanced over at the stove, I could tell by mashing a few beans with a spoon, they were getting about half-way done. At once I flipped the knob which controlled the burner to low. Succeeding this, I quickly whipped the next largest kettle I could find out and proceeded to fill it to the brim with the little grains of white rice. Next I covered the rice with small amounts of water, thinking, *That should be enough.* With one quick twist to the knob, the burner was set on high. *Everything is going as planned, no mishaps will happen this time.*

About this time, Mrs. Bent called me wanting to know if she could borrow a nice lace tablecloth. I found the prettiest lace tablecloth I had and went to her place. Somehow we got on the subject of hopping johns, and to my amazement, she had never heard of them called that and only knew them as black-eyed peas. Truth be known, it was amazing to find someone who had never heard of them.

We stood on the porch chatting away for a few minutes. I didn't want to take up to much of her time because I knew she was busy getting ready for this, "Big feed." Indeed, I was almost ready to leave when my neighbor with flaring nostrils turned to me head on, I smell smoke from somewhere. "Don't you?"

I turned on my heels and saw the smoke pouring out of my open kitchen window. Oh my gosh, it's coming from my kitchen.

We both raced upstairs to find the rice was everywhere and in flames. It stuck not only to the top of the stove where it laid in a circle of fire, it had flowed out of the pan and onto the front of the oven door where some was spilt on the floor. We were both coughing as the air was filled with cloudy dark smoke. The fire was proceeding quiet rapidly even to where chunks of the on-fire-rice fell to the floor. I frantically stomped them out as Mrs. Bent asked the stupidest question I ever heard in my life, in the mist of the place on fire. "Where is your baking soda?" I just stood there with my mouth opened and pointed to the small cabinet next to the stove.

I didn't think baking soda made much sense so I had my own ideas. I reached for a cup and filled it with water and threw it on the fire. It seemed to ignite it even worse than it was already and I jumped away swiftly. Mrs. Bent told me she knew what she was doing and had put a few stove fires out herself, so to just stand back. So I did. There was a burnt-sugary smell heavy in the air and I felt dizzy from it, so I leaned upon the next available cabinet and, watched wide-eyed. Sure enough, Mrs. Bent did know what she was doing and soon the fire was reduced to smoldering bits of black rice. Dusty white powder, from the baking soda settled on everything which had been burning. She proceeded to explain to me, important instructions on how to put out a stove fire, never use water, only baking soda.

Mrs. Bent, with her thirty-year-old wisdom, set me down and explained how to cook up a pot of good rice. Sometimes, during the conversation, I felt like she wanted to tell me what the surprise dinner was going to be. But she held out and didn't. Though I was dying to know and wished she had. When the lesson was over, I realized how blessed I was to have a neighbor who was so helpful.

Later, after the mess was cleaned up, I put on another kettle of rice, as per Mrs. Bent's instructions. It was a success this time because I realized how rice triples in bulk, and you have to add a lot more water to the pot. I poured it into a special dish spreading the black-eyed peas and fatback over the top. My biggest worry now was hoping my husband wouldn't smell the smoke. Of course he did, but he pretended not too. Lucky me! Lucky too, in the sense which there was a throw rug I had put at the foot of the stove, so the fire did not damage the tile in any way, only the rug.

My husband, Billy, and I, were invited into the living room of the Bent's residence but were stopped just inside the living room. Mr. Bent graciously held a white cloth napkin over one arm and stepped toward us, bending over from the waist as he spoke, Please come this way. I will show you to your table. My husband and I looked at each rather surprised. Surprised he was dressed in clothes resembling a waiter, and even more surprised, he was acting like one. We followed him at his request till we came to the dining room doors. When there, he stopped abruptly, Please wait while I open the dining room doors so you may see this "Big feed," together.

At that moment it dawned on me, that this could have something to do with my husband and I being newly weds. But there wasn't much time to think about it because before you knew it Mr. Bent opened up the dining room doors into the most elegant picture in which to lay your eyes upon. It was more then I could believe.

Right before us were tables elegantly decorated with red and white tablecloths. There were candles which glowed and smack dab in the middle of each table were cooked crabs piled high. What a delight and surprise. My eyes felt as big as saucers as I glanced over at Billy. I couldn't tell how he felt as his face seemed to show no emotions and he certainly did not say a word. There were many fine salads and foods of every kind imaginable, which surrounded the mountains of crabs on each table. I stepped forward and placed my hopping johns dish on one of these tables. Man! Oh! Man! What a delight and surprise for me. Though I had eaten crabs many times before, I had never seen so many at one time. Crabs were my favorite kind of sea food. I just couldn't believe it. My mouth watered and I couldn't sit down fast enough.

Before I could pull the chair out to sit down, I looked up at my very quiet husband. He just stood there in utter surprise with his mouth wide open and his eyes averted downward scanning the feast set out on each table. By the look on his face, you would have thought something horrible was on the tables. Yee! Gads! Can you believe what happened next. He grabbed my arm angrily, with all his might, and knocked the chair over, in which I had pulled out to sit down on, and one of the tables with the crabs on it, fell over too. Everyone was astonished to see the chair and the table topple over, and my husband dragging me forward to the front door. No one knew how to react to his angry behavior. Everywhere I looked in the room, people seemed to be trying to be nice about the whole thing and asked me to sit back down. They said to Billy, "It'll surprise you how good crabs are. Really they are so good."

While everyone was trying to remain calm and clean up the mess of crabs which had spilt on the floor from the table, I said, "Oh come on honey! Try them you'll like them. "Boy! Oh! Boy! That was the wrong thing to say! He got even more riled up, and squeezed my arm tighter as he pulled me out to the porch. Unreal, ridiculous, crazy, out of this world kind of behavior. I wished he would have been pleased with the feast. Because we had only been married a short time, it was hard for me to understand this kind of behavior. It was embarrassing to me! I had never in my life experienced anything like this. I didn't know how to react or what to say.

He wasn't through with me yet. He shoved me through the door with a mighty push, grabbed me to keep me from falling. Shouted in my face. "NO! Wife of mine is going to eat anything like that! The next thing I know you'll expect me to eat them too! Don't ever even think I'll eat things like that! It's the most disgusting thing I have ever seen. You get your purse and we will get the hell out of here, and never again will we have anything to do with these crazy people. Don't ever let me catch you talking to them, you hear?"

To me they seemed very fine people. They were only being kind to us. I thought, because we were newly weds. All the same I nodded my head at my husband in agreement. He knew I would do what he said. Although I thought to myself, *he doesn't know what he is missing. And if I want to eat crab, I'll just do it when he isn't around.* All I wanted was to have a happy family, no matter what the cost. To this day, I realize there were many things I did out of fear I didn't know what my husband might do, if I did not agree with him.

The tone of our marriage was set at this crab feast. Most of the time afraid to speak up for myself and give my own feelings on things. Part of the reason, or maybe all, I despise confrontation of almost any kind. Especially with an overbearing and verbally abusive husband. There were happy times too, I can't say there weren't. But sometimes I wonder today, if I had stood up for myself at the first confrontation at the crab feast, if our marriage would have been different.

On the other hand, I've heard it said, hard times builds real character. I do believe it must. Really in my life it has built real character. Now I feel I don't need any more character, really I don't and that's the truth!

God does not give us any more than we can bear.
But I wish He wouldn't trust me so much!

Quote by: Mother Theresa

THE BLIZZARD OF 49

In the winter of 1949, the Midwestern part of the United States experienced an extremely severe winter. There were blizzards for days and the temperatures dropped to way below minus zero. During this period of time, I lived in northwest Nebraska. The countryside here has few trees and consists primarily of acres and acres of rolling hills. In the summer time, if you gazed out across these rolling hills, you would more then likely see hills of corn fields and plentiful heads of cattle grazing.

It was during this particular hard winter of 49, when many cattle ranchers lost their cattle because of low temperatures and, high freezing winds, and snows. Military planes were brought in to drop hay to keep the cattle from starving to death. The planes would fly over the fields, and pastures, and drop hay bails near as many cattle as they could. Montana, North and South Dakota, Minnesota, Nebraska, and other States needed help from this severe storm. Some of the ranchers lost all their cattle, while others were lucky enough to receive the flown in hay-supply, just in time to save their herds.

Most of the ranchers sent their school age children, in the winter months, to live with families who lived in town. The children usually stayed on for around three months to attend the town schools. We took care of three of these country children in that winter of 49. The town's café, which we owned and operated, was our house.

One morning, I looked out the large front café window and saw how hard the wind was blowing and how much snow had accumulated. I never saw snow pile up so fast. In some places the snowdrifts had piled up more than fifteen feet high. The snow was coming down at an angle and so thick you could hardly see your hand in front of you.

It was just before dark, when my husband and I heard, not far off, the roaring engines of cars stuck, it seemed in snowdrifts, trying to get out. My husband hurried to put on his winter clothes. When he left the house he looked like a mummy with only his eyes and mouth exposed. The snowfall had slowed down until visibility was much better now. I was thankful. At least my husband could see where he was going and wouldn't wonder around lost. As many times reports of people lost and frozen to death had been in the news of late.

This particular day, the temperature had dropped to 34 degrees below zero and the wind was blowing forty-miles an hour. It doesn't take long to freeze to death in this kind of weather, even with visibility being better. So I prayed, that the people, and my husband, would be able to get back to our warm little house which was connected to the café we owned.

My husband found three cars full of people. They had tried to plow their way through snowdrifts several feet high and now all vehicles were stuck. These people were from northern Minnesota and were traveling to the next town to attend the funeral of a relative, when they were hit by the storm and plowed into snowdrifts. One of their cars had developed a water hose break which in turn immediately froze it up. The rest of the cars were hopelessly stuck in the snowdrifts. They knew they were stranded, and in danger of freezing to death. They were relieved when they saw my mummy-looking husband, who appeared out of no where. We gladly opened our doors to them.

Our three children, and the three country children we were taking care of, my husband, myself, and the twelve adults from the three cars which we had just taken in from the blizzard, were all now crowded in our little house. There were twenty people in all. Two things were in order. One to feed them and two, to find places for them to sleep. There were not enough blankets for everyone, so my husband made a roaring hot fire to keep us all warm. Some of them slept on the floor, while others curled up in chairs to sleep.

In the winter, when there was a big blizzard, usually the phone and electricity would be out of order. Most people in this little town, in those days, didn't have inside toilets. When the weather was severe, everyone had to use, what is called a bed chamber. At this time, I had an extra bed chamber because my grandmother had given me one. It is a large pot with a lid and it is used just the same as you would a toilet. When it is full, it is dumped in the outhouse after the storm is over.

To get water for bathing, cooking, and drinking, the men went outside and hard packed snow down to the rim, into a big round tub. The kind used to take baths in. Then, two men would heave it on top of the wood stove to heat for water. Because we had so many people in our home during the blizzard of 49, the men would have to fill the tub often.

On the fourth day, our food supply had almost come to an end. All of which remained in the cupboards were, flour, salt, and baking powder. The severe winter had caused the chickens to stop laying, and my canning goods had disappeared altogether. Therefore, it was not unreasonable when three of our men, decided to go hunting as soon as there was a break in the blizzard. They knew their best bet would be ring-necked pheasants, as the country had an abundance of them. They also knew they needed to bring back lots of them to feed twenty people.

So it was the next day, the sun appeared bright and early, chasing away all other clouds, and our men took off in their wintery cloths and warm boots. There was a nearby corn field with bushes in places where the snow had blown away. It was where they needed to go first, since pheasants are lovers of cornfields. Soon, the men were carting in their arms, nine chocks they'd shot. They did this all within two hours. They told us how they did this. They would walk along the fence line and scare the pheasants up, while the others would aim and shoot.

When the men came home half-frozen, some of the women cleaned and cut up the pheasants as fast as they could. Then, they put them in the hot cookstove, while still other women made bread dough to bake. The aroma of baked pheasant, filled the air, and soon we were smacking our lips with its delicious taste. The storm raged through the night but in the morning the sun came out again and our hunters went out again and brought back eighteen fat pheasants to cook. The pheasant-hunt happened everyday in which the weather would allow it.

After three more days of this dreadful storm, our phones were repaired. Our phones were the crank-kind back then with at least four or five on the party line. When the phone rang all the people on that party line rushed to the phone to listen in. It truly was a blessing in those times when there was one call, and nearly half the people in the town knew how everyone else was getting along.

The happy day came when the sun stayed out all day and it was so bright, it hurt your eyes. That same morning, the people from Minnesota left in their cars, following the snowplow which passed by our café. They followed it all the way to the next town. The days cleared up after that, and the winds subsided, and life became normal in our part of the country. And soon, as far as your eye could see, there were cornfields waving in the summer breeze and cattle grazing on a thousand hills.

HUNGRY COYOTES

I lived in a nice quiet little town in the northwest part of Nebraska. Winter in this part of the country, many times meant blizzards and freezing temperatures.

One day, I gazed out my front room window at the bright sparkles of snow. My thoughts turned to the bright snow laden hills, how peaceful it looked. And how, at any time another blizzard could hit and ravish the area. Our home was behind the only café in town, in which my husband and I, owned and operated.

At this time Gala, a neighbor girl asked, if I really wanted to go skiing with her that night. She was excited about the change of weather and excited about her skiing adventure and had just depicted a pack of coyote tracks in the snow. Realizing this particular harsh winter of 1949, in which Nebraskans were now in, had left the coyotes exceptionally hungry. Of course, immediately she raced home.

Gala thought it unsafe to be out there alone. Then she thought, with two or more people, things would be different. Gala said, "Coyotes would never attack them." I agreed with her, therefore I decided to go. Besides, because of the blizzard, we had to close our café and I had some free time. It was soon settled I would ride over to her house and we would ride double to the hill in which we planned to ski on. The only other problem was, I did not have a pair of skis. Soon we remedied that problem and decided to ski double on one pair of skis.

Flash my horse, was in the shed behind the café, as he should have been. My husband had shoveled some snow during the blizzard to clear the snow from the door. We needed to get in to feed Flash. Yes, again earlier the wind had blown snow drifts in the way of the door. I hurried off to fetch the shovel and haul away the collected snow. Finally the snow was cleared away enough to open the double doors and I was able to bridle and saddle Flash. He was raring to go! He could out run most of the horses in that neck of the woods. Or at least, I thought so. Jumping on, with the vitality of a twenty-four year old, I pulled the reins the way I wanted him to go, and said, "Hey, Flash, let's go to Gala's house." And off he galloped in a dead run. I slowed him down enough to veer around the snowdrifts and sometimes just to enjoy the view.

Here we were going to Gala's house just as the sun was going down. On the opposite horizon a gorgeous round moon rose shining as if it was trying to outdo the sun. And I guess it did. It was darker now as I approached Gala's house. I started to holler for her in the cold and crisp air. It seemed my voice carried for miles.

Gala did not come out, so I figured she didn't hear me. I tied Flash up close by, though I knew there was no need too. If I told him to stay, he would have stayed as long as I needed him too. He was that sort of a horse. I knocked on the door and when Gala answered, I came in and rushed over by the fireside to warm myself, as she put her boots and winter clothing on.

As soon as Gala was ready, we hurried out the door where Flash was waiting for us. Gala brought in one hand the pair of ski's from the barn while carrying a rope in the other hand. They were rather oldish in style, given to her by her grandmother. You could tell Gala was proud of them and took excellent care in often polishing the hickory wood surface which jutted out in both the back and front from an unusual binding of sorts. She tied the rope in a fashion on some of the flaps on the saddle. Then swung each rope around each side of the saddle in back of the horse, and knotted their ends to a wooden sled she had drug out from the side of the house.

We went as fast as we possibly could, considering the conditions on the snowy ground and the small sled with the skies dragging behind us. At times, it was a little difficult to get around the high snowdrifts but we made it. It was a good thing Flash was as gentle as a lamb and didn't mind such shenanigans. Once Gala stopped to make sure the knots were secure. At last we came close to the hill where we planned on going snow skiing, and veered Flash toward it.

Once at the hilltop, fresh coyote tracks were visible everywhere. To my dismay, Flash started to prance around showing off with the little sled knocking and banging around him. He was frantic, but we finally managed to calm him down and swung off of him. We found a nearby clump of trees where we tied him up after undoing the sled which had trailed behind him. You could tell he was nervous, his nose twitched, his ears were all held up high as if listening to something, and his tail swished back and forth.

Gala and I cast our eyes out yonder over the hill and than, scanned the horizon. The moon's bluish-tints crept over the snowy ground, like long fingers in the night. Kind of a forbidding cast, like we shouldn't be there. The only sounds heard were the crackling of the crisp-ice over the snow and the swishing horses tail. Otherwise, it was quiet and eerie. It seemed as if the whole world had suddenly stopped. But we were determined to have some fun, so we shrugged the spooky feeling off.

It was freezing cold as we both tried to hurry to get on the ski's. We managed to fumble around a lot until we finally did it, gloves and all. Gala had heard the coyotes howls the night before, in the very same spot in which we stood. And for some reason, I suddenly remembered a news report from last winter about an old fellow who fell in the snow, and was attacked by hungry coyotes. And when they were done with him, there was hardly anything left. I also heard, after they knock you down, they go right for your juggler vein. Goose bumps rose on my arms and neck, and I tried to calm myself down. Of course Gala and I were young, and could get away. After all, I was only twenty-four and Gala was only eighteen. So what was I worried about anyway?

Gala had handed me a narrow silk-sash to tie myself onto the ski's behind her. And I held onto her waist as Gala pushed us off with a pair of long ski poles she had brought. Steam rolled out of our mouths as we flew down the hill. We didn't get far and, we started to laugh. We thought it was so ridiculous, two people on only one pair of ski's. We laughed so hard we fell over. The sash had fallen clear off my feet by now and, luckily, Gala knew to release the binding leathers on the boots so she wasn't attached to the ski's, before we rolled part-way down the hill. Glancing up at the horse, I could see Flash as he just stood wide-eyed watching us, as if he thought we had lost our minds. He was holding his head high, as if he were very important, too. We got up and brushed ourselves off.

We retrieved one ski each and climbed back up the hill for another run. We positioned ourselves accordingly, repeating the first rendevous. Gala pushed off as before with the steel poles, and the evenings silvery shadows fell on us like it was a poetically lovely night. Our attempts were not far along when we lost control again and, we fell yelling and, laughing at our great fun, even if we weren't making very much progress. This time though, after which I took the sash that bound me to the ski's, Gala loosen the bindings and allowed the pair of ski's to slide the rest of the way down the hill. Steam rolled out of our mouths, as we watched them hit the bottom of the hill.

We had nearly forgotten about the coyotes, when a sudden outburst of animal yowls, froze us solid as ice, right where we were sitting. Then answered howls followed from a place somewhere on one of the nearby hills. Looking to the south, we saw what looked like eight dark specks moving like shadows against the silvery moon on the hilltop. They were heading in our direction. They were coyotes, we were sure of that.

Flash thrashed around, pulled at the reins, stomped, and whinnied, as we raced as fast as we could toward him. Unexpectedly, Gala turned on her heels before we reached the top of the hill, saying she needed to get the ski's because if there was another blizzard tomorrow, she would never find them. She slipped several times and fell many more times going down the hill, but continued. I called out to her several times to come back, but she just kept on going, sometimes sliding on her behind and sometimes rolling down the deep snow. I could see the coyotes getting closer and closer racing across the rolling hills towards Gala. I screeched at her and pointed in their direction. "The coyotes are coming close to you." She did not answer but kept on going.

My only hope was to get Flash, swing around the clump of trees, and go down the not so slippery pathway, and hope I can make it to her before the coyotes do. By the time I got Flash, he was hysterical. Soothingly I talked to him and calmed him down some. I knew it had taken too long to do this, but I had no choice. Flash didn't want to stand still, so I had a hard time getting mounted. I talked to him again and told him about our situation and about the coyotes trying to get Gala. It worked. I finally got a foothold on the stirrup and swung around on him.

I rode as fast as possible across and through the snow. Sometimes I thought Flash would slip and fall but he was as sure footed as a mountain goat and kept on going with no incidents. When coming to a clearing, I heard Gala's horrified shrieks. It seemed to crack the frozen-air right before my eyes where I set on top of Flash. I dug my heels into Flash's side and we slid around the corner. Then I saw it, the coyotes were circling all around her. Some of them pounced and snapped at her boots than jumped back into the circle from which they came. I dug into Flashes sides again, knowing we had to get there fast, and also knowing, the only hope now, was to scare them away. Flash bulked strongly but finally he gave in, and I let him have the rein as he pushed his self forward against the heavy snow. I looked helplessly at Gala before me in the distance. *God help her*, I cried to myself.

Flash slipped down on one knee, somehow I found my voice to prod him on and he struggled up. I was thankful, it didn't appear as if he had hurt himself. I knew I was lucky he didn't go down all the way. Two more coyotes leaped at Gala, then, jumped back in line. Some of the coyotes backs were tinted brownish-colored from the silvery moon's cast. While yet others which faced me, had red-eyes which flashed and white teeth which snapped from snarled lips. I heard Gala's screeched yells and saw her hands flung out in front of her, Go away. Leave me alone.

With a choked cry I hollered, Hang on Gala, I'm coming. Really, I wanted to yell and scream and wave my arms to scar all the coyotes away, but I was afraid it would panic Flash and he would buck me off and leave me there to be eaten too. I had to remain calm, I kept telling myself.

Flash and I were almost upon them now. The coyotes looked up at us with wild flashing red-eyes and gnarled teeth. My heart was in my throat. Fear enveloped around my throat as if strangling me. I gulped hard. Then, as if by a miracle, they backed away, all eight of them, and ran off. Later, to think about what happened, I was amazed that Flash didn't panic at the sight of the wild beasts. It was a miracle. When I got to Gala, she was trembling like a leaf. Tears were streaming down her face as I swung off of Flash. We embraced each other for a moment in tears, than, after confiscating the pair of ski's, we climbed aboard flash. She carried the ski's under her arm until such a time we were able to make it up to the top of the hill and attach the little red sled so the horse could drag it behind him.

Slowly we made our way to our homes across the night snow of the Nebraska's almost tree-barren slopes. Gala escaped being eaten alive and I felt if it hadn't been for Flash and someone watching over us from above, we both would of never escaped alive. Once at Gala's house we put her ski's and sled in the red barn and she hurried into the house waving good-by from the door jam.

The funny thing is, Flash became friskier than ever all the rest of the way home that night. Once he stopped abruptly to see me, I am sure, fly over his head into a snowdrift. I was positive I saw a smile form on his horse mouth. For he looked as pleased as he could be. But he did not run away. Instead, very swiftly and quietly, he scooted himself over so he was rubbing up against the high snowdrift I had landed in and waited patiently. It seemed to me this horse was sure one intelligent horse. He knew what he was doing. I got up, brushed myself off and I stepped right into the saddle, easy as you please. I guess that is what you call, horse fun.

I decided to reward him by singing all the way home to him, "Old Mac Donald Had A Farm." Flash was the happiest horse in the world to get back in his warm shed and, who knows, maybe even to get away from my singing. And just maybe, he really did understood what was happening on the hill that day with the coyotes, because he really did do his best and he really was the one that saved Gala and I from the coyotes. To me, he will never be just any ordinary old horse.

THE FEROCIOUS RAT

Our first home was in the Midwest. Like so many when first married, we did not have the money to buy a home or other things we wanted to have. We made a deal with the landlord to fix up his house for most of the rent. It sounded good, until we saw the old house. There was nothing we could do except do this job for the rent, unless we wanted to live in our car. Winter time would be too cold for us. If you saw this house you would not believe it. It was built in 1885, and at the time we moved in it was over sixty years old. It had not been taken care of for over thirty years. At one time it had been a beautiful home for someone. Both front and back porches had fallen down, and most of the windows were broken or completely gone. The roof leaked, the foundation was decaying. To top that off there had never been any plumbing. What a way to start our married life. This was going to be a challenge.

We were thankful the landlord was going to furnish most of the material. There was so much to do we hardly knew where to start. There were many things we thought should come first, such as an indoor toilet.

Both my husband and I had to find ways to make a living. He did odd jobs and sometimes he would be gone for a few days. We tried to earn money any way we could to help ourselves. We grew our own garden, and I sewed for others, crocheted, and made caps, blankets, and scarves to sell. Sometimes I would iron for others. Anything we could, we made and tried to sell.

After a while the house began to look better. We had torn out the back side of the kitchen to get ready to install an inside toilet. In the backyard there was a very healthy apple tree loaded with apples. Past the apple tree a little way was a creek where you could see the animals drink water. Standing in the kitchen, looking into the distance, it was pleasant to watch the birds and animals. Since I made delicious apple pies, I decided to bake some to sell. In order to gather, peel, and make the pie crust before dark meant I would have to rush. The two pies I completed would have to sit on the table until morning. It was not the way I wanted to do it, because hot apple pies are the best.

A few days before, we had bought a few baby chicks. The weather had turned cold so we brought them in the house and put a towel over them to keep them warm. They were too young to take the cold nights.

The next morning when I got up there were no baby chicks in the box. There simply was no sign of the chicks anywhere. Then looking to where I had put the two apple pies, I saw nothing on the table. On the floor were two empty pie pans. What had happened to the apple pies? This couldn't be! Maybe a cat or dog had come in the opening in the kitchen. The only thing I could do was to make some new pies. I needed to get them baked before dark, because I would not have time to bake them the next day. I also had to close the opening in the kitchen, so the cats or dogs couldn't get in to eat my pies.

The next morning I got up early so I could go sell my pies. I hurried to the kitchen eager to begin the day. This was unreal! Looking at the table where I had put the pies, again there was nothing there, and looking on the floor were two empty pie pans.

Ridiculous! As I picked the empty pie pans off the floor, I spotted a huge rat scurrying away. What would I do? A little mouse scares me to death. To see this huge rat in my kitchen was simply too much. YEA GADS! It couldn't go out the door because I was standing near it. Of course my mouth was wide open screaming. I grabbed the broom to chase it out, but instead the huge rat ran into a corner. I took a whack at it, and to my utter surprise, the monster rat jumped at me. I took off running as fast as I could without looking back, yelling at the top of my voice like a maniac. Our closest neighbor lived only a hundred feet from us. When I got to her house, I left out the part about the rat chasing me, and only told her about the disappearing pies. She said they were river rats. She let me borrow her rat trap and showed me how to set it to catch the rat.

IF YOU ARE WEAK IN THE STOMACH, IT WOULD BE BEST TO FINISH THIS STORY HERE. UNLESS HOWEVER, YOU REALLY WANT TO KNOW THE GRUESOME DETAILS:

The trap went off during the night. When I hurried to the kitchen I was shocked. The rat was trapped by its hind leg. The poor thing! There it was wriggling and trying desperately to get out of the trap. What a struggle it was having. So pitiful! I scooted the trap near the opening in the kitchen, then pushed it with the broom to the opening, gave it a big whack, and out it went, right into a mud puddle. Right away it started to slowly hop, trying to get out of the mud puddle and break free of the trap. Before I could put the broom away, it had escaped the mud puddle and scrambled into the thorn bushes. I was really happy it was gone. Now I could make apple pies without that particular rat eating them. But what if there were more rats where that one came from? We would have to get the bathroom finished as soon as possible. There was no way I was going to sleep at night until the bathroom was finished.

The next day I went into the backyard where the thorn bushes were. Nearby was the rat trap with part of the rat's hind leg still attached. It had gnawed its own hind leg off. That poor rat!

ROCKY MOUNTAIN OYSTERS

Growing up on the East Coast years ago and then marrying a Midwesterner man was sure to be a totally different kind of life for me. You betcha it was. At the time, I could hardly wait to get started with the Midwestern life. All my life I had wanted to live way out in the country and ride horses. Since I loved horses so much, even though I had never ridden a horse, I was sure it would be easy for me to learn to care for the animals, and I was dead set and determined, to have the best riding horses anywhere.

Never in my life did I realize how hard it would be to become a real country girl. There was so much more to country life than I had imagined. Even though I had gotten books from the library to read about horses and other farm animals, it was a whole other story living on a farm and taking care of them.

The first years I got into the swing of things. We had sheep, cows, chickens, two riding horses, a dog and a cat to take care of, but no hogs. I definitely fell in love with country life. All the work and hardships were worth it just to be able to ride the horses. The feeling of being on a horse when you are racing through a field with the wind in your face, or trying to cross a small river with the water splashing around you, is indescribable. There is nothing to compare to this kind of experience.

We had lived in the country for a year when a wealthy attorney came to our door.

Of course we invited him in. Most people in the area knew the attorney. He said he wanted to get acquainted, and he invited us to his Rocky Mountain Oyster Fry, which he held every year not far from where we lived. Having lived near the ocean most of my life, I missed sea food, especially fresh fried oysters. It would be a real treat for me!

Our neighbors told us what a huge event this Rocky Mountain Oyster Fry was. The attorney had a tradition of inviting anyone and everyone to come and enjoy this event. He furnished a band, all the food, drinks, and didn't allow any kind of alcohol at his Oyster Fry. There would also be dancing, swimming, horseback riding, singing, a horseshoe toss, and games for everyone at this event. Every year all the farmers for miles around took most of the day off for this big event. They would talk about it for weeks ahead of time and plan what they were going to wear. They came early to brag about their animals and crops to each other. These hard working, happy, and hardy people enjoyed life to the fullest.

It was customary for some of the women to show off their special dish at the Rocky Mountain Oyster Fry, each trying to outdo the other. Most of the women made special Western style outfits to wear at this affair. Many farmers gathered together beforehand to practice singing spiritual songs or putting on a barber shop quartet.

Soon the Rocky Mountain Oyster Fry was only a few days away. I decided it would be a good idea to go fishing the day before the event, so I could show off how I fried fish. The day before the big party, we went to the wild Missouri River not far from where we lived. We always had good luck where we planned on going, and usually always caught sturgeons and channel cat and bass, our favorites. This day was no different, and we caught all the fish we needed. I was so excited about the large sturgeons we had caught. We could bring caviar to this exciting party. It would be a good treat for everyone there. When you clean sturgeon, the first thing you do is to take out its spinal cord, then skin it, collect its eggs, and fillet it.

The party was the next day, but that night for our dinner, we rolled some of the sturgeon, channel cat fish, and bass in pancake flour with just a little cornmeal and salt, and dropped them in hot oil for a short time. Boy! Oh! Boy! It is some good eating if you like freshwater fish. We saved some of the fish and all the sturgeon eggs, so we could take them the next day to the big shindig. The only thing I knew about caviar was, it's supposed to be special.

After dinner was over, I decided since we wanted to leave early the next morning so as not to miss anything, I would prepare the caviar before going to bed. The fact is I really didn't know how to prepare the sturgeon's eggs.

Just thinking about tomorrow, my mouth was watering for the fried Rocky Mountain Oysters, never questioning any difference between them and the Eastern oysters I had always eaten. They were bound to be good, one of my very favorite sea foods.

IF YOU DON'T WANT TO LAUGH, PLEASE DO NOT READ THIS:

Before preparing the caviar, I sat down to give it some thought. I didn't think no one would want to eat raw fish, would they? I just couldn't imagine it feasible to eat raw fish. These sturgeon eggs must be prepared the very best way possible. Smothering the eggs in pancake flour wouldn't do, boiling them seemed out of the question. Nothing sounded like the best way. Maybe frying them in plain hot oil would be the best way to prepare them, or maybe I could bake them. Baked fish eggs! Oh, no, never!.

Finally, I decided to drop them into hot oil in a pan without a lid on them. I didn't want to smother them. After dropping them in the hot oil, I quickly turned my back for a few seconds to do something else. LO! and BEHOLD! Suddenly I heard a loud and clear pop! pop! pop! pop! and more pops! Before I could get the lid on these little black naked eggs, they were popping out all over the stove and floor. And amazing thing, they were white on the inside. Just try it some time and you'll see. Be sure the oil is hot before dropping them in!

Now I was in a real dilemma, because I had told one of my neighbors if we got sturgeon, I would be bringing caviar to the Rocky Mountain Oyster Fry. I thought it best she didn't know what I did to the caviar.

The next day we got our cowboy outfits on and went to the big shindig. It was time to forget about the caviar and to enjoy the wonderful party, with its singing, dancing, swimming, ball playing, horseshoe toss, and other games. OH! Such fun for everyone. Once in a while you could smell the hog farmers' animals when the wind was blowing our way.

Now it was time for the men to start frying those delicious oysters they had been bragging about. It was about all I could do to just sit there, my mouth watering in anticipation. It wasn't quite the smell of the oysters I had eaten on the East Coast, but the smell was so very good it didn't matter.

Everyone was getting hungry and thirsty, and sat about drinking soda pop trying to be polite while waiting for the oysters to be served. Someone started to sing Yankee Doodle Dandy, and was clapping their hands to keep time with the music. Right in the middle of the song a loud voice yelled out, "Come and get it!"

In a few moments a long line had formed. Finally, it was my turn in the line to be served. I was given eight or nine of something I thought were a little smaller than East Coast oysters. I popped one in my mouth and thought, these are very good, but they don't taste anything like East Coast oysters. I popped two more in my mouth this time, thinking maybe that would make a difference. They tasted good, but they still didn't taste anything like East Coast oysters. I was puzzled. There was no way I could keep quiet about this. The next thing you know, I bellowed out loud and clear so everyone could hear: "These oysters are delicious, but they don't taste anything like East Coast oysters!"

I could not believe it! Everyone busted out in a very loud laughter. I couldn't imagine what was so hilariously funny about East Coast oysters. Then I began to feel embarrassed, not knowing what I should be feeling embarrassed about. I tried my best to laugh along with them, but it was a weak laugh feeling like a knuckle brain, stupid, outrageous, scatterbrain, out of touch, whatever it was, I felt it all.

A farmer and his wife were sitting next to me. He asked his wife to explain to me in plain English about Rocky Mountain oysters. Meanwhile he and some of his buddies had a knee slapping, belly splitting, laughing good time. Man! Oh! Man! What in this world could possibly be that funny.

Even though I was extremely embarrassed, I could hardly contain myself. No oyster I had ever eaten had caused this much hilarity. I didn't think it was one bit funny.

The wife hesitated and stuttered some before starting to tell me. I said,"Tell me, tell me! What in the world are these men laughing about?" At last she explained what Rocky Mountain oysters are. You see, they are not oysters at all. When a farmer raises pigs for the market, he has to neuter them while they are young, except for a few he saves for breeding.

The farmer's wife explained that those tables a distance from the others were for people who didn't want to eat the Rocky Mountain oysters. They were eating another part of the whole pig that had been roasted with barbecue sauce smeared on every once in a while.

My neighbor never asked me about the caviar I had promised to bring if we caught sturgeon. I was relieved because I didn't want her to know about the mess I had made of them. My goal now was to find out how caviar was supposed to be prepared. To my amazement I found out they are eaten raw. Such was the education of a city girl becoming a real country girl.

FLYING SAUCER HAIRCUT

I grew up in a large family in the south. I was the only one of eight children with red hair. Although my hair was more of a dark red, it stuck out like a sore thumb and I preferred to call it brownish red. All my life I wanted to have raven black hair and dark brown eyes like the rest of my family. My family and others picked on me often. My nickname was "hot head." Everyone seemed to think when I got angry I should act on it, although in our household you were never allowed to get violent, it wasn't allowed in our family. Civilized citizens used their brains, we were told over and over.

Back in the days when I was growing up the elderly were respected and above all you respected your teacher. Each student tried to go the whole school year with a perfect attendance record. If there was a conflict in school, your mom had a conference with the teacher to get to the bottom of the problem. If you had been bad in school, the problem was, when you returned from school you were in double trouble. It seemed to me my mom always took the teacher's side of the issue. Not that I was one to get in trouble much.

It was about time for me to be my own boss. You! Betcha! I'll whack off some of this God-awful reddish hair. Back than most people took pride in how they looked. It didn't matter how I fixed my hair, it was noticeable.

Finally, I was out on my own. One of the first things I did, as soon as possible, was to cut some of this horrible reddish hair. The sooner the better. I grabbed a pair of scissors and sat in front of a mirror to decide how short I wanted it. I wanted it shoulder length now, so I cut away in the front first, than started cutting the back. I checked the mirror as I cut, but no matter what I did, the back of my hair remained a total mess.

I had an interview for a job in only two days! What was I to do? I had gotten married to have a family and my husband was out of work. It was urgent and necessary to look my best for the job interview.

When I told a friend about ruining my hair, she came over to straighten it for me. The interview went very smoothly, and I obtained a job working in a 300 bed hospital. I worked in admission and took care of patients insurance. This was exactly the kind of work I enjoyed and gave it 100% all the time. In just a few months I realized it was the kind of work I loved, and it was my purpose in life. I could do some good helping and it made me feel good inside.

While working at the hospital, a decision was made to form a Personnel Club for the employees. After working there one year, imagine this, twenty out of the twenty four departments voted for me as their president. What an honor! I was floating on air to think they chose me as their president. It proved to me that hard work really does pay.

There was no choice for me. It was either work or go hungry. My husband had a drinking problem and usually didn't come home until the bars were closed. When he did come home he was usually drunk.

I tried to get help from ministers, Anon, psychologists, psychiatrists, and even his boss. But all the effort expended trying to help him was fruitless. The only person who could help him was himself. That's right! Really, I wanted to help him if possible. When I had called his boss, my heart was fluttering with anticipation. It was a real let down to learn his boss needed help as badly as my husband.

When I was first married, I excused his drinking, not knowing he was an alcoholic. Over forty years ago there were two choices, in situations like this: Either live with him or leave him. Of course, with money it would have been easier to leave him and raise the three little girls alone. But with him out of work much of the time, it seemed there was never any money. Getting a job was the only choice I had.

My family was two thousand miles away and all of them were struggling to raise their own families. There was no one to turn too. Anyway, I didn't want anyone to know about his horrible rages and verbal abuse.

It was a challenge just to stay alive and get the necessary things. When not at work I spent every minute I could with our girls, trying to make up for the verbal abuse and showing them the good things in life.

Desperately needing a car, I started making pillows and baby sitting after work when my husband wasn't home. I saved every penny I could, doing without anything not necessary. With almost enough money saved, I looked for a real old car that would be cheap.

When I finally found one, I asked the owner to save it for me until I could save enough money to buy it. I was thankful I almost had enough now, because things were going from bad to worse and I absolutely had to have a car to get to work faster.

One hot afternoon, I decided our little girls and I would walk over a mile to the family who had the car for sale to tell them I almost had enough money to buy their old car. We were in a hurry to get there and back before dark in case my husband came home early. Perspiration was dripping off all of us, I do believe this family had compassion on us, even though they didn't know our circumstances. They decided to drive us home, and on the way we discussed the old car I wanted to buy. He said it needed to have the carburetor repaired. If my husband could fix it, he could get the car for us tomorrow. I told him I'd have to talk my husband into letting me have this car first. He said, If it will help you, tell him it's yours if he can fix the carburetor.

Finally, I talked my husband into letting me have this old car. He really didn't approve of me working but, he knew he'd have more money for him to drink, so he gave in. Thank God!

It was an old jalopy if ever there was one! It stuck out like a sore thumb. You would have thought it was a brand new car the way I was carrying on, strutting around like a proud peacock. Now I wouldn't have to take the bus one-and-a-half hours to work and one-and-a-half hours home. What a relief! Now happy as a lark, because I could be home with our girls more.

Rushing to work, I'd park it at the very back of the parking lot, then hurry to the front door, hoping no one would think it was mine. Actually I was very proud just to have even an old clunker. Living with an alcoholic or drug addict you are lucky if you have anything. Right! When he came home, it put me under a tremendous amount of stress. I didn't sleep well, and felt like I was up against a brick wall. For sure, if you don't have a problem you can't solve it, and as far as my husband was concerned, he didn't have a problem. Being responsible for our children, I wanted them to enjoy life and tried as best I could to let this happen under the circumstances.

As president of the Personnel Club, my goal was to make the hospital the very best in the city. Everyone who worked at the hospital seemed to have the same goal. It was a joy to work with this kind of people.

When my year was up as president of this club, a decision was made to have a Suggestion Committee. They appointed me as chairwoman. The Suggestion Committee was formed in order to improve working conditions in factories and large companies including our hospital in the city. The plan was for the workers to feel free to write their praise or critique of where they worked with or without signing their name. The boxes would have locks on top of them with slots for you to drop-in your suggestions. Everyone was so excited about getting started.

Working hard on the plan with all the confidence in the world, I decided to call the newly built Air Force Academy located in Colorado Springs, Colorado and make a reservation for a luncheon. To get this Suggestion Committee started, I needed as many people as possible involved. Each of the ten places I called for a luncheon happily accepted the invitation.

Everyone agreed we should start early so that we would have a chance to tour the Academy. It was a once in a lifetime opportunity.

My old jalopy could not possibly make it to Colorado Springs from Denver, where we lived. So, I made arrangements with my secretary to ride with her. We were going to go earlier than the other ten people.

The night before the luncheon, my husband came home earlier than usual, drunk.

I was afraid to say anything and hoped he would go to bed and sleep it off.

My reddish-hair was a little longer than I wanted it. I decided to cut it a little shorter. Maybe it would not draw so much attention. I absolutely had to look my best for this fantastic mission.

Just as I started to trim a little hair off, instead of going to bed, my husband came in to where I was trimming my hair, grabbed the scissors out of my hands and started whacking off my hair. LORD! HAVE! MERCY! What could I do? Quickly I said, I only want a little cut off and I can do it myself.

Angrily, he said, "A little, nothing! You want it all cut off, you know."

Again I tried to reason with him, but to no avail. He would not listen, not at all. I knew if I resisted there would be a knock down, drag out fight. Guess who would be the looser? Me, of course.

He stopped whacking on my hair for a minute. Man! Oh! Man! And I breathed a sigh of relief. It was to good to be true. Never in my life could I have ever imagined in my wildest dreams I'd let him whack away at my hair when drunk. I was feeling hysteric, but had to contain myself.

Will I have any hair left? The whacking continued until the only hair left was above my ears. In other words, on the very top of my head. Can you imagine how I looked? My hair shaved up above my ears and a little reddish-puff on top of my head. I knew very well when I looked in the mirror, I would look ridiculous. The result was unreal, unbelievable, horrible, and out of this world. LORD! Have mercy! My hair looked like a flying red saucer. That being a little round bump on top. Could anyone be more embarrassed? I don't think so.

Everything was set and we were supposed to be in Colorado Springs early the next morning. How could anyone call off a meeting of this kind with these important people? Since I was the hostess I'd have to do my best. Breaking a promise has always been a no-no in my book.

81

Can you imagine standing up in front of important people making a speech with this hair cut? My career would be ruined. My stomach was turning and I wanted to cry. Then, out of the blue, came a thought. Would the world come to an end because of this hair cut? NO! I think not. But how could anyone make such a fool of themself?

Walking to the front of the Academy I pretended not to be embarrassed. It wouldn't work. The situation was impossible. I wished I had a scarf to put over my head, but knew it would not be cool to wear a scarf to such an elegant luncheon. How stupid to even think of such a thing. Maybe I could crawl under the table. That would never do would it? Suddenly, a cadet came to lead us into a fantastic, dream-world dining room. Because they were treating us like royalty, it made it a little easier to act like my hair was normal.

My secretary started toward the cocktail room behind the cadet. She was taller, and I figured, maybe if I stay close behind her, my hair wouldn't be so noticeable. I hoped her height would conceal this God-awful hair. Of course, it didn't conceal my hair, but it did relax me for a few minutes.

I knew nothing about ordering any kind of alcoholic beverage, and I didn't want anyone to know I had never ordered any before. I'd had enough embarrassment already with my horrible flying saucer haircut. Look at this flying saucer haircut, I surely wouldn't have to drink to make a fool of myself. Would I?

Thinking quickly for a moment. Surely, if everyone else was ordering mixed alcoholic drinks, shouldn't I? I decided my solution would have to be when the cadet came to serve us. I would slowly turn my head as if there was something important in the opposite direction. That would force my companion to order first and I could say to make mine the same as her's. We were almost the last ones to be served, because I wanted to be in a corner away from the others. I was trying very hard not to be conspicuous.

My secretary ordered an Manhattan. I never knew there was such a drink, but I pretended I knew, all the same. She drank hers down and ordered another while mine was only half-gone and I was beginning to feel it's affect. I sat there sipping very slowly, and some of the time only pretended to be drinking. I didn't know what to do. If I drank anymore, I wouldn't be able to make a speech that I'm suppose to make. Should I accidently knock the glass over? Then, have them fill it again, and I could continue to pretend to drink. Or, should I run as fast as I could out of the place so I wouldn't have to make the speech?

Being against a brick wall, so to speak, I did some deep thinking. Then, out of nowhere came this brilliant idea. Listen to this! I'll slide her empty glass to me and my half-full glass to her. Yes! I do believe that will work, if I'm careful not to let anyone notice. How do you like that for a slick solution?

Just as I slid my half-full glass to her, this loud mouth said, WHAT! As if she wanted everyone to know. Quickly, I gave her a hard kick under the table. Thank-God, she understood what the kick was all about. Otherwise I would have slid under the table if she had said more. I didn't think I could take much more embarrassment. This could have been a real disaster.

Then I started to worry about her drinking. She had already had two more drinks and wouldn't be able to take notes if she continued. GOOD! GRIEF! What could I do?

She ordered another Manhattan. She gulped down my half-full glass, and was ready to gulp down the one she just ordered. Was there a way out of this horrible mess and still maintain a bit of dignity? Sophisticated was out of the question. Flashing through my mind came this disastrous thought. Hey, why don't I jump up awkwardly and accidently knock over her Manhattan. Then I could rush to the ladies room with her so I could give her a good chewing out. This all has become ridiculous. Yes! We do have to get this over with quickly.

At this point, I thought dying would be easier then making my speech with this ridiculous, unreal, and horrible flying saucer haircut. How in this world could anyone look sophisticated and know what they are doing, looking like this. Especially looking like this and being a lady. You have to remember this was back when women did not wear their hair that short. Still, after all this, I was determined, not to give up. Anyway, the world won't come to an end, will it? Although I felt like it would that day.

My stomach was gnawing away, and my heart racing along full speed, when another idea flashed through my mind. Yes! This will work. I could race out and break a leg or fall off a chair and pretend to have a heart attack. NO! It would never do to try anything like that. In the first place, it would not be right, and in the second place, I wasn't a good actress. That's right! My mind was racing to find a solution to fit the occasion. And it finally came. Humor was the answer. OH! Yes! Why hadn't I thought of this before.

Slowly, after the luncheon I got up, taking a deep breath and hanging onto the chair with one hand to steady myself. Gripping the chair harder as I put my other hand to my hair. There was total silence.

Gracefully I stroked my hair lightly, than loudly, pretending I had confidence, I said, How do you like my flying saucer haircut? My only thoughts than were to lighten things up in the room, everyone's faces were so rigid.

Deep-down, my next thought was to run out of this place as fast as my legs would carry me. Another dead silence. It seemed like eternity. Then, an statue-looking cadet, turned his head and laughed. The rest is history. Everyone in the room, all at once, let out roars of laughter. And the rest of the cadets that were there, joined in. Some laughed until they almost cried.

It will always stick with me how things can appear to be extremely horrible, awful, ridiculous, and terrible, and yet sometimes, it can turn out to be extremely good. That's life! It sure is.

IT'S A MYSTERY

Long ago when I was young and lived in a city, we had a neighbor next door who had three children. She would come quite often to have coffee with me. I was so busy, I could not sit down very long at a time. She would sit and watch me work four or five times a week. For the life of me, I could not figure out how she could get her work done. There were two boys and a girl which I thought were hers. They were about eight, ten, and eleven years old. They were never allowed to come to my house to play. Who I thought was their mother they called Carla, and who I thought was their father, they called Ottis. Carla's husband worked at a mental hospital as a male nurse.

One day Carla said, "If you buy some material I will make you a dresser scarf." She knew I did not have scarves on my dressers. A few days later, I bought the material and gave it to her. She brought the scarf to give to me a few weeks later. It sure looked beautiful on the dresser. I thanked her, and in appreciation for making the scarf for me, I gave her a few quarts of my homemade bread and butter pickles.

One day while she was at my house, my husband came home drunk. Earlier, while I was cleaning the house, I had moved a chair a few feet from where it usually sat to clean behind it. Noticing it had been moved, my husband started to yell at me in front of Carla. She jumped up in a hurry and went home. Before she got out of ear shot, she heard him scream at me, "Don't you have any brains! Can't you think! What's wrong with you!" I knew there was no way to make him understand. I wanted to explain that I was cleaning the room and didn't have time to put the chair back, but I said, "Oh! I should have moved it back where it belongs. I am so sorry." After a few more outrages he settled down and fell asleep on the couch.

In those days there was no help for people with drinking problems. I could have left him! Sorry, not me! Not with little girls and an emotionally ill boy and no place to go. I realized there was something wrong inside with him and with me for putting up with it. The only one to help him was himself.

Carla came over the next day. She could not understand how I could put up with his outrages. Then I got the shock of my life! Out of the blue, she said, "I know how you can kill him. You can put something in his coffee and no one will know it." OH MY GOD! How could she say such a thing, or even think such a thing. It was all I could do to hold my temper. I felt if she was that kind of person, I had better stay calm. Calmly I said, "Listen to me. I don't ever want to hear such talk in front of me again. Please keep this in mind." A few weeks passed and the conversation never came up again.

One day Carla and the children were gone, and Ottis was at work that day. The mailman left some of their mail in my mailbox. My intention was to drop it in their mailbox, but I thought I would knock before dropping it in their box. A lady opened the door very slowly and shyly. I had never seen her in the three years we had lived there. I asked her name, and she said, "Sara." I said, "Have you been here long? I have never seen you before." She said, "Yes, I have been here over five years." Handing her the mail, she refused to take it saying, "I am not allowed to touch their mail or anything else of theirs, not even their dishes. I wash my clothes by hand and I am not allowed to go outside."

I really did not know what to say or think. After a few more minutes I asked her if she had thought about going to the police about this. She said, "I don't know how I can with this situation."

I was really puzzled. Going back home, I tried to think of what I could do for her. Sara stayed on my mind for the next few days. I hurried over to her house the first chance I got when everyone was gone. I wanted to show Sara the scarf Carla had made for me. She had done such beautiful work. Showing the scarf to Sara was my excuse to find out why she was a prisoner there. I told Sara what a beautiful job Carla had done on the scarf. Sara looked surprised and puzzled for a moment, then said, "Carla! She didn't do the work on that scarf! I did every stitch of it.

"I cannot believe Carla would try to make me think she did the scarf!" I hesitated because I had more than I could handle at home, but I told Sara I would try to help her, even though I didn't have the foggiest idea how.

The first chance I had when everyone was gone, I went over to Sara's house again. She told me why Carla was holding her prisoner in her home. She had married Carla's brother, and Carla thought it was her fault he had died, but he died of a heart attack Sara explained. Carla's brother was a gentile and Sara was a Jew. Carla and her husband Ottis sent Sara back to New York from where she had come. But Sara's folks would not keep her and sent her and her three children back to Carla and Ottis to live.

Carla had made me believe the three children belonged to her and Ottis, and the way she talked, I thought the children loved Ottis.

Early one morning a truck pulled up to their door. The children, Carla, and Ottis were rushing to throw things in the truck as if it was trash. It seemed they didn't have one thing packed, and everyone was hurrying as if they only had minutes to move. I asked the youngest boy where they were moving. He said, "I can't tell you anything, but it's not far from here." The day before they moved, Carla came by my house. She didn't look well, nor did she act herself. I asked her if she was okay, and she said, "I don't hurt. I guess I'm okay."

A few weeks passed from the time they had moved. The youngest boy called and said Carla had died. Of course, I asked what had happened. The boy said she had been sick for a few days, but did not go to the doctor. The boy told me what time the service would be and where the mortuary was. It was only a couple miles from where we lived. Maybe since we were neighbors, I should take some flowers.

When I got to the mortuary Ottis was standing next to the casket with his back turned to it. He was so pale I thought he was going to pass out. He started to turn to look in the casket just as I grabbed him to keep him from falling down. Knocking the casket over would not be so funny.

Trying to make him feel better as I grabbed his arm, I said, "It's a good thing..." But I stopped before I could finish the sentence. He braced himself against the casket. Hanging on to him with all my might, to keep him from falling over, I said, "Let me go get help for you."

Firmly and angrily, he said, "Absolutely not, no way. I will be all right, just give me a minute or two."

I wanted to make sure he was okay before I did finish my sentence. (It's a good thing I waited.) Now finishing, I said, "It's a good thing your children love you so much." At this he jumped up and ran out the front door.

One day, a couple weeks after Carla's death, all three children came to my door. To my utter surprise, they confided that Ottis had something to do with Carla's death. They said Ottis had put something in Carla's coffee over a period of time, which they were sure of, but felt certain they couldn't prove it, so they didn't want to tell anyone.

I told them that I thought they loved their dad. To my surprise, they said he was not their dad and that they hated his guts and hoped to never see him again. They wanted me to tell them anything I could about Ottis to use against him. There was nothing I knew about him, and there was no way of proving anything. Although I have thought of this incident many times, I still don't know if anything else could have been done.

NEVER GIVE UP

When living in the city, I was worried about our boys who would soon be teenagers. I was so afraid they might get into some kind of gang. So we decided to move to the country. We felt there would be so much more freedom in the country and more work to keep them fit in mind and body. Just think of all the fishing, hunting, swimming, and hiking they could do. And they could meet other active people. For their spiritual up bringing, the church would be smaller and the people would be more like family. Everyone would be acquainted with each other.

We were all excited about looking for a place we could afford. Believe me, that was very hard to find. Seeing nature in the country side after living in the city, the stars were more sparkly in the evening and the sun's illuminations bathed the trees and land more brightly by day. It's beauty was more than anyone can describe. It was absolutely fantastic, to feel the freedom of the country.

At least we found something we could afford a few miles out in the country. It was surrounded by forests, lakes, and mountains. A beautiful little creek ran through on the backside of our property. How lucky we were, we wouldn't miss our city life, and we could always drive to the city for the things we needed.

The two boys helped us make plans for all the things we wanted to do on our new property. They were already making plans for going hunting, fishing, swimming, and hiking. The first year we had to plant trees and make a garden as soon as possible. The first step was to rid the virgin ground of the rocks and to clear an area large enough for the garden. The ground needed to be plowed, the seed sown, and we had to devise a way to bring enough water to the garden. Nothing was going to deter me from raising a garden.

I gazed proudly at my first garden planted in the beginning of the season. All to soon, I found it to be a complete flop, a disaster. The rocks and the bad soil, had taken its toll. It could hardly grow. We had been looking forward to all the healthy food we would have soon and, now, our hopes were dashed. But never would I give up. No! Never!

The next year rolled around and I toiled once more for my little garden in the woods. It still was skimpy. By the third year, I fully expected to have a fantastic garden. I became more knowledgeable on gardening and even found a few gardening tricks I claimed. One of them was, NEVER GIVE UP.

I was as happy as a lark when getting things ready for this garden, this time. It was such a pleasure to plant all the good things and watch the garden grow. This third year's garden looked beautiful in the middle of July. All the lettuce, cabbage, cauliflower, and broccoli, looked robust and perfect in their tidy little rows. Each plant was getting little heads on them. I had spent many hours and gallons of sweat to get it weeded. The family could hardly wait for this organic food to be ready to eat. Waiting was every bit worth it, though.

Each day I was delighted to get up bright and early to see how much everything had grown. One particular morning I went out almost in a run to look at our beautiful garden. My mouth opened wide in utter surprise. I beheld a sight which froze my heart solid, for just a moment. All the tops of the lettuce, cauliflower, cabbage, broccoli, and many other plants which were planted had been destroyed. What a disaster!

We lived in an area where bears, skunks, cougars, foxes, raccoons, and lots of deer abounded. It was obvious one of these varmints had come in the night and destroyed the plants.

The next year came, and my garden was looking better than the years before. I went out to do some work in it. Lo and behold, there were two deer just leaving. I peered at the neat little plant rows and found every one of the tops of the vegetable plants were missing. GOOD GRIEF!

I had an idea for the next year. It would fix them up real good. This mixed up concoction, I am thinking of, will make them want to leave my garden for good. I will put together a mixture of hot pepper, garlic, and something they like to eat, oatmeal. Yes, that should work.

The next year arrived and I planted as always. The little plants sprouted quite nicely. Then it was time to apply the concoction I had planned earlier to keep the deer at bay. Each plant was carefully wiped with it.

The next morning I caught the deer coming out of my garden. To my amazement, they were smacking their lips like they were eating candy. They seemed to really enjoy the hot mixture I had put together. It wasn't working.

Earlier, I'd found out our only hope to keep animals, such as deer out of a garden, was to erect kind of a fortress around it. An eight foot fence, to be exact. We couldn't wait any longer, we had to put one up soon. Whoa! Wait a minute. Did I say we? My husband was not a farmer nor was he an outdoors man. So I didn't expect him to help me.

I rose up the next morning with an enthusiasm you would not believe. I believed I could conquer putting up the fence by myself, as I had done many other projects on my own on our little farm. So, I went after it full force.

First, I measured and squared the garden off and thought as I worked. *It is better my husband does not know how hard it is for me to do this.* I dragged the ladder over along with the sledge hammer, and kept busy most of the day. Going up and down the ladder dragging the heavy sledge hammer with me each time to pound the posts in the ground.

I had hoped I would be able to pound some posts in the ground before my husband came home. I had only managed one so far. There was one consolation I was sure of. I was strong from all the exercise I'd done on our farm and, therefore, it gave me assured confidence that I could do it.

Many hours passed by and the sun was sinking in the horizon. The job would have to end soon. At least for that day. I had many more posts yet to drive into the ground. And there had been delays, so far, because of the boulders in the ground. When I would hit one, I would have to climb down the ladder and dig it out, before I could continue.

Dirt kicked-up on the little road to our house in the distance, and I could see it where I stood on the top of the ladder. I knew my husband was coming. My heart was in my throat, as he drove up and walked around our country house to get where I was. He didn't say a word but just stood there and watched me for a while as I went up and down the ladder. Two posts were solid in the ground, two feet down and I was proud of them.

I knew I should quit, but I wanted to show my husband how easy it was for me to do this job. So I attacked one more post. Of course it had to have a big rock in the ground to dig out first. Which I tried to act like it was an easy thing to do, when in reality it wasn't. I had to struggle to get the hard ground broke but finally I did. The boulder was the biggest one yet and I had to dig deep around it till I was standing in the hole with it.

My husband, Billy, took one step closer to me and peered down at me in my little hole I'd dug out all around the rock. I still was frantically shoveling dirt out of the hole when I heard him say, "I could have told you they have metal post drivers you can buy at the store. Don't you know nothing?"

I could of shoveled a load of dirt right on his toes as he stood there, but I didn't. I just wiped the sweat from my brow and, not wanting confrontation, smiled. Oh, really. I guess I better go down and purchase one right away.

The metal post driver was not what I thought it would be. It was not automatic but it was somewhat simpler to use than a sledge hammer, and shovel. I was excited about it though. I could hardly wait to drive the first post with it. It was such a treat to hear the metal clinking on the metal post.

The fence was up many days later, and it protected the garden from the deer very well. And, I found, after a few years of mulching and fertilizing it, our family was rewarded abundantly. My motto, never give up, paid off! The garden produced vegetables beyond what you could imagine. Even to the point of when people happened to pass by our garden plot in the woods, you would see them smile and say, "It definitely would make it to first prize in a garden contest."

THE AMAZING LITTLE GOPHER

Years and years ago when our children were very young we decided living in the country would be best for our children. Where we bought our country house was gopher country. Never in my life had I heard of nor had I ever seen this little creature we would be sharing our land with. Therefore, we were in for a few big surprises, as growing a garden with our own vegetables was very important to us.

How fantastic it would be to see the little plants grow from tiny seeds into large healthy plants. What a miracle this is to me. Getting them to produce like you want is a whole different story, especially when you don't know much about gardening. You can get fantastic results if you know what you are doing.

First the soil composition has to be just right for what you sow or plant. Then the water, sun, and shade must be appropriate for that particular seed or plant, and each plant has to be in the right spot. Every little thing is very important. On and on I could go about a garden. There is no end to learning about gardening. This subject has cultivated my mind and I have a better understanding of many things because of it. As a never-give-upper person, I knew some day I would eventually have a fantastic garden. Each day as the plants grow and develop, it is amazing how alive you feel when you see the results of your labor.

One day, when I was standing near a tomato plant, I saw it move. YES! I was absolutely sure it moved. Moving closer to see what was causing it to move, I stood very quiet and still for a few minutes. The tomato plant started to sink. What was going on? Was there a hole or a hollow place where I had placed the plant? The next day I went to see how the tomato plants had grown. To my amazement the plant that had moved the day before and another one had completely disappeared.

YE! GAD! After two more days there were only four healthy tomato plants left out of the twenty-four I had planted. HOLY COW! It is the gophers! YES! SIREE! I do believe it is what they call gophers destroying my garden. So much of my work had gone down the drain. My job now was to try to save the remaining plants.

My neighbor said everyone had the same problem with gophers. Instead of asking how to get rid of them, I figured surely I was smart enough to take care of the problem. After all they are smaller than I am. WRONG! I never realized what a challenge it would be.

My first idea was to put a little towel in the gopher hole to plug it up, even though I feared it could smother them. Rolling the towel up, I pushed it down the hole. It disappeared. Yes! It did!

What now? Maybe I could pour gas down their holes. NO! That would never do. It could blow up or burn you. You never know what they might have in their living quarters to take in a towel and many tomato plants down there. Maybe I could jump up and down on their home. No, that would never work either. I couldn't bring myself to do such a cruel thing. Besides, a grown lady jumping up and down on the ground where the gophers unseen home is. Ridiculous!

A few days later every single tomato plant had disappeared. Noticing they did not pull down even one of the marigold plants, I decided to put some of the marigolds down their hole to see how they liked that. Of course, they did not touch it.

One neighbor said to put hair down their holes. So, I even whacked off some of my reddish brown hair and put it in their hole, wishing it was redder so they could see it better. They left my hair alone and continued to destroy my garden plants. Even though all tomato plants were gone, I had hopes of saving the other plants. I didn't want to put traps out for the monsters. That seemed too cruel and could cripple them. LISTEN AND LISTEN GOOD: But was it not cruel for the gophers to destroy my garden. OH! YES!

All of a sudden it came to me. Maybe I could get rid of them by pouring water down their hole. YES! SIREE! Right into their home. I carried pail after pail and poured it down their holes. It disappeared as fast as I poured it in. Faster and faster I ran with the water. It was getting ridiculous how much water was going into their home. Maybe the water hose would work better. Monte, our two-year-old boy, was trying to help. He loved to watch the water disappear down the hole. Of course, sometimes he missed the gopher hole, and hit my face with the water! Oh! What fun.

The gopher hole was never going to fill, so we stopped for lunch. I shut the water off and while going in the back door decided to leave the door wide open, so Monte could go in and out. After lunch, I went outside, and turned the water hose on full blast. By now there should be a small lake under our garden. I stood there motionless, waiting to see the gopher families swim out. I wanted to get a good look at them. After spending hours waiting, I decided to give up.

Hearing a noise in the hallway, I did not think it was important. Monte came into the front room where I was working, yelling and pulling on my leg, jumping around trying to tell me something about a gopher. I followed him into the hallway, and there to my utter surprise, was a little gopher standing on its hind legs with its little paws up to its dripping wet face. It was squeaking and going around and around as if calling for help. HOLY! COW! How pitiful the little creature looked.

This amazing gopher couldn't stay in our house, of course, though Monte was eager to help it. I grabbed the broom to push the amazing little gopher out the back door.

Finally, with a little help from me, it flew out the open door and raced toward its home in my garden, happy as it could be to get away from me, I'm sure.

From that day on, as long as we lived there, it was a constant royal battle with the amazing little gophers.

IT WAS SUPPOSED TO BE FUNNY

In the western part of the United States of America, we struggled to make a living on a wooded mini farm. It was our choice to live in the country. We feel this is real life, even though it is harder than some city life. In the fall we decided to buy a couple milk goats. My husband agreed to buying the milk goats, even though he did not enjoy country life as much as I did. It was not his kind of thing. He did like any kind of challenge though. For some people a challenge is to produce something. Building a goat shed for the goats and putting up a seven foot high fence, 75 by 75 feet was right down my alley. The goats now would have plenty of room to jump, leap, run, hop, and bounce all over the place. It would be so much fun for me to watch these curious, happy, animals. Jumping, bouncing and leaping. My husband reluctantly did agree to help.

The winter months are usually snowy and rainy in this part of the country. We needed to get the goat shed and the high fence finished before winter. The weather was already starting to freeze at night.

Fall was in the air. The trees were changing color and the stars were sparkling in the cold night air. If we bought the goats before we had a pen for them, they would eat things they shouldn't be eating. To top that off, these happy animals will follow you in the house and make them selves at home. Of course, they may make a mess of anything in their path purely for the joy of having fun.

There wasn't much time to get this job finished before winter. We squared off our plot of land for the shed and fence. A big truck pulled up to deliver all the material in one trip. My husband did not seem like he was having very much fun. On the other hand, I was so enthusiastic, it was hard to wait for the job to be finished. Checking to see if we had all the material for the fence and shed, we noticed there was no lock for the gate. These type of animals need a very strong, special lock.

We decided we would wait until we had the goat shed and fence finished before going back into town to get this lock. After working long hours for a few days, the shed was built and the fence near enough finished to start making the gate. While my husband was finishing the gate, he wanted me to go in the pen to the back and pick up the rocks and put them in a little pile near the back of the high fence. In the meantime, he finished working on the gate and began installing it in the opening. While I rushed around picking up rocks, I heard him hammering what I thought to be plenty of 16 penny nails

95

in the gate. Then to my surprise, I saw him hurrying to get into his car and race away. I never suspected why he was in such a hurry.

Exhausted, tired, and cold, I hurried over to the gate, expecting to run home as fast as I could to get in out of the cold. I grabbed it with both hands, expecting it to open. But no! Not even a budge. I pulled, pushed, yanked, and banged to no avail. This was supposed to be funny! Oh! Yeah!

The fence was very strong with hog wire four feet high and three strings of barb wire at the top and one string at the very bottom. There was no way I could climb over the top, and the bottom was out of the question. I knew my husband would be gone until the bars were closed. Realizing it was up to me to figure a way to get out before it got any colder, I decided to try to dig under the barb wire at the bottom of the fence.

With nothing but my hands, some sticks, and a rock for digging, I started to dig. Needless to say, it was very difficult. My hand started to bleed, the sticks kept breaking, and the rock was a poor digging tool. It was taking forever to dig a hole deep enough to slide under. No such luck as a quick job. I just had to keep digging, first with the rock, then with my hands, even though they were raw and bleeding.

I tried again to slide under the barb wire and again it was not quite deep enough. It was getting very cold out and my fingers were getting stiff. I refused to give up, knowing it would be another few hours before my husband would get home. I could be half-frozen to death by the time he got back..

Finally the hole was just large enough for me to slide under. What a miracle! Thank, God! Once out, I quickly reached an arm back under the fence to pull the dirt back into the hole I'd dug to hide all evidence of my escape. The fence was only about one hundred feet from our house.

Exhausted, I made a beeline straight to the house, and grabbed a bite to eat because I hadn't had time to eat all day. Then I showered and jumped into bed as fast as I could, hoping I would make it before he got home. It was almost time for the bars to close and he would be home soon. I thought if I pretended to be asleep, he wouldn't say anything. But! No! Not him! He just had to wake me up. Of course, I was not asleep. He persisted, so I pretended to wake up. Sleepily I answered him with a weak "Yeah". He said almost in a shout, "How did you get out of the goat pen?" I said softly, while crossing my fingers, "It was easy." The whole thing was supposed to be funny for him, but I would not give him the pleasure after what I had gone through. To this day, he does not know how scared I was nor how hard it was for me to get out of the goat pen. My attitude now is that very few things are impossible to conquer.

CALMLY WAITING FOR DEATH

My older sister was in charge of the younger children, and when I was about five years old she read us a story about a mule and another story about a scorpion. She read many other stories, but these two stuck in my mind. The story about the old man and the mule taught me you can't please everyone. The story of the scorpion left me with a lasting fear of any kind of insects. Once when I became frightened on seeing a praying mantis, she said, "Honey, it's praying for you. You don't have to be afraid of insects."

The story she had read to us was about a scorpion stinging a little boy who then died an agonizing death, with foam coming from his mouth. My sister made this story so scary, I had nightmares about it. I'd never seen a live scorpion, and I thought they must be vicious and deadly. The story stayed on my mind for years.

Later when I was married and grown up, we moved to an area where there were scorpions and other insects I had never seen before. We were starting over on a plot of land that was so thick with trees and bushes, it was a struggle to walk through them. Needless to say, it was going to be more than the challenge of a life time. We looked around to find the best spot to build our home, after which we had to make a clearing big enough for a house.

This place made us feel like real pioneers. We worked long hours clearing and cleaning patches of land large enough for a garden, house, outhouse, and barn. All the trees we cut down had to be replaced in spots where we needed shade. The dream of seeing this land with a home, barn, and garden all finished with landscaping, inspired us. Our spirits soared as we thought about one goal after another.

Our first task was to dig a well and build a pump house. After we finished the pump house, my plan was to build shelves in the new pump house. So many things could be stored on these shelves. I knew very little about building shelves, yet it seemed to me that it should be a simple task even a child could perform. Frankly, I wanted to show my husband I could do things he could do and maybe a little better. Putting every effort into this exciting new task, I went full speed ahead. I took great pains to measure each board to the fraction of the inch, then measured again just to make sure. There were going to be no mistakes making these shelves.

After getting one shelf finished, I stood back to inspect it. Boy! Oh! Boy! This was the finest shelf anyone could build. I stood there for a few seconds

98

admiring it, smiling from ear to ear, as proud as a strutting peacock. Grabbing an old rag to wipe the sweat off my face and to wipe my hands, I decided to take a break, because now I was certain I could build shelves as good as anyone.

While sitting eating lunch, I daydreamed of all the things I could build. Before going back to work on another shelf, I decided I would move an old rotten log. I kicked it over, and there on the ground lay a family of scorpions. This was the first time I had seen a scorpion. In a flash the story my older sister had read to me about the little boy who had died an agonizing death from a scorpion sting flooded into my mind. It was easy to decide that this family of scorpions would not be in this world for long. I was prepared to send them to glory land as fast as possible. Now that I knew what a real scorpion looked like, I would be on the lookout for them.

With the scorpions dead, I went to continue with my shelf building. I drove in more and more nails to make sure these would be the strongest shelves ever built. Missing the nail once in a while, I hit my fingernail or sometimes my thumbnail and had to stop temporarily because of the pain. But I never thought of giving up, even after three black and blue nails and several curses! I had driven enough nails in these shelves to build a battleship. One shelf built and the next one almost finished, Man! Oh! Man! Things were looking good. Now I was ready to build a chicken house, hog pen, barn, outhouse, and a fence without any help. I'd show my husband what I could do. My mom always said if you want anything done right, do it yourself. Now I had proved that's the way to do it.

After hammering the last nail into my fantastic shelves, I decided to drag some boxes over to the pump house to put on the shelves. After putting three of the boxes up, there was room for one more box. I decided to give it a heave ho. This box was a little heavier than the other boxes, and it was about all I could do to put it on the shelf. GUESS WHAT! Just as I got it on the top shelf and let go of it, all of the shelves came crashing down with a loud bang. How could this happen? This was impossible! I was sure I had driven enough sixteen penny nails into these shelves to build a battleship. I couldn't believe my eyes. I was embarrassed and dumbfounded. Completely defeated now, my heart sank to think I had to face my husband after acting like such a smarty and know it all. Sure, he heard the loud bang and noise as the boxes descended to the floor and he suspected what had taken place.

I walked up to him very shyly, hating to say anything, but I badly wanted to know how those shelves could all fall with so many nails in them. I had to wipe tears from my face as I tried to muster up the prettiest smile I could. I stuttered and stammered trying to tell him what had happened but he already had it figured out. He tried to listen as I told him how I had hammered many, many nails securely in. So why, why, why had every single shelf fallen down.

My husband had a smirk on his face as he bust into laughter. Very calmly, after he had finished his loud, knee slapping belly laugh, he told me, "I could've told you screws and bolts are much stronger than nails, and it's the way you drive them in that counts." Why hadn't I thought of this? Screws and bolts were a whole other ball game for me.

After this dent to my ego, I wasn't about to put myself through more humiliation. Because the shelf building had turned into such a disaster, I felt sure my husband would not ask me to help with any other carpenter jobs. Still, there was so much to get done before the rain came, which we expected in the next few days.

Maybe I could build a wooden box to put the wood in for the winter. Surely a plain square box would be easy enough. Two of the sides I put together turned out just fine, but when it came to the other sides, I just couldn't make the square. The boards were slightly off and the nails were too big. This was an unreal and unbelievably out of shape box! This box was hilarious, and yes, for me enough humiliation. You would think I had learned from the shelves. No way! Not me! But I really did have it figured. I was absolutely, positively sure now, I am not a carpenter.

After the house was built, all the boxes were finally carried in, and there was lots to do getting everything in place. My husband said, "Since you know now you are not a carpenter, maybe you would like to help paint the outside of our new home." Wow! Oh! Yeah! I'd like to paint, surely anyone could paint.

Everything was going very well. I had one side of the house almost finished. But even though I had a long sleeve shirt and my hair was covered up, there was paint on my hands, shoes, nose, mouth, and spots here and there on my clothes. Oh! Well! I don't have to be so careful now since I'm already spotted all over with paint. Now I can fly along at full speed ahead. I'll get this job finished much faster.

You always start at the top of what you want to paint. Since this house had a high roof and I was going to paint the trim first, I set up a tall ladder and carried a gallon of paint up to the top. I stood below the paint and as I reached to get some paint, the whole gallon of paint tipped over and went right down the inside of my blouse. Lord have mercy! What a shock! Then I counted to ten rather slowly, then counted my blessings, because it could just as easily have spilled on top of my head instead of down my blouse. I also felt lucky I hadn't fallen off the high ladder when the paint came down on me. It could have been a real disaster.

For the first time we were going to sleep in our new house. Our spirits were soaring at all we had accomplished in the past few months. On this particular evening the clouds were getting darker and rain was pouring with much lightning. We were so thankful we had all our boxes safely inside the house and some of the things in them had been put away. Building a house is very hard work, so you get tired and fall asleep as soon as you hit the bed.

This first night in our new home, I fell asleep for a short time, but then woke up, and for some good reason had to go all the way out to our outhouse to do my business. You know what I mean. It was three o'clock in the morning and pouring rain. With my old lantern in hand, I tried to hurry, racing around to find an overcoat to put on. Afterward I went back to bed, but I didn't sleep after I had done my business. In a short time I had to get up again. It was about three-thirty now. It was still raining, and I hated the thought of going outside again. Just as I was reaching for the overcoat again, I felt a sting on the bottom of my foot. I started to scream, but didn't want to wake anyone at this hour. With the light from the lantern I saw a scorpion on the floor. Flashing through my mind was what my older sister had read to me when I was very young. I grabbed a shoe and sent the scorpion to glory land, then placed it where the family could see it so that after I was dead they could see what had happened to me. Very calmly, I sat there awaiting my fate. I wasn't going to wake up my family because I thought no one could save me and I didn't want to alarm them.

I waited one hour, then another hour, and another. My foot was starting to swell, but there was no pain except for the place where the sting was. Analyzing my situation, I figured that with no phone and at this hour, it would be hard to get to a doctor. Of course, what was the use of going to a doctor if you are going to die anyway. As time passed, and I still wasn't dead, I thought, maybe, just maybe, scorpions are not as poisonous as I thought they were. Looking at my foot, it was still swelling. Well, I'll just have to sit and wait calmly until daylight arrives, and if I'm not dead, my family will take me to the doctor. It seemed so strange to be so calm in this situation.

101

Fanny Louise Smith

When the family did get up, they rushed me to the doctor. After checking my foot, the doctor said, "Unless you are very old or very young, these Oregon scorpions are not poisonous to most people." I thought I might be something special because I wasn't dying an agonizing death.

THE THREE REAL BEARS

It had been a beautiful, mild summer, but fall was approaching quickly. We lived in a small town in the country on five wooded acres by a small river. We maintained a small apple orchard, kept chickens, and maintained a large vegetable garden.

One day in late fall, a friend from the city came to visit us. She loved country living and small towns, so I took her around the valley shortly after she arrived so she could see our little valley. On the way home, we stopped at the local market and bought a few groceries. There was a lot to catch up on, so we talked nonstop as we lifted the groceries out of the trunk of the car and carried them into the house. We didn't stop talking until it was well into the night and we could hardly keep our heads up when we finally retired to bed.

The next morning, as my friend walked by a window, she was shocked to see a huge black bear tearing apart one of our apple trees in the front yard. It must have weighed 500 pounds, and it wasn't hard to see how he came to be so large. He made a real pig of himself as he gulped down all the apples he could reach.

As we watched, he climbed up onto our porch and walked up to the sliding glass door, testing it with his paw and than sniffing at it. We stood transfixed, afraid he would push against the door, or even lean against it and it would collapse.

The year before, I heard about a bear which had broken into a house not very far from ours. He destroyed everything in the kitchen, ransacking it for food. We had been told that if we looked a bear in the eyes, it would charge us, and the very last thing we should do is run away from it. All these things came flooding into my mind as I watched the huge black bear checking out our house.

As quietly as we could, we ran around the house closing the drapes so the bear couldn't see in. We talked in whispers as we peeped through the drapes to see what he was up to. All day long we watched him patrolling our property and tearing down our apple trees. As night approached we all hoped the bear would leave and go back to it's den to sleep.

We waited till way into the night and then decided to hazard lighting a kerosene lamp. As we stumbled around in the darkness, trying to remain as quiet as possible, we began to realize how ridiculous our situation was. The more we bumped into things, the funnier it became. We started to laugh.

"Shush," I said, "We have to be very quiet."

We would try to be serious, but then would burst out laughing again. The more we tried to hold it in and keep quiet, the more we laughed. Finally, utterly exhausted, we decided to go to bed, hoping everything would be normal in the morning.

The next morning we quietly got up and peeped through the drapes. Lo and behold, not only was the big black bear still there, but he had brought his whole family as well. There, standing only a few feet away, was mother bear and her cub.

I feel like Goldilocks and the three bears, I thought and began to picture myself in her shoes. *If this were a fairy tale, I would gladly fix these bears the very best of food and they would peacefully go away, appreciating the great hospitality I showed them.*

The bears in Goldilocks, however, did not tear down perfectly good fruit trees. My three bears destroyed everything which stood in between them and food. They were extremely dangerous and I certainly didn't want to anger them in any way.

I knew these bears were trying to fatten themselves up and, the way they were eating everything in sight, I didn't think it would be long before they had all the fat they needed to make it through the winter.

I had parked my car about twenty-five feet from the front door. We knew we couldn't get to it without being seen by the bears. All we could hope for was that they would soon get tired and go away. We waited throughout the long day and all that night, but the next day they were still there.

The next morning the papa bear began sniffing around the trunk of the car. As we watched, he raised up on his hind legs and dropped his huge paws down onto the car. I wanted to scream, but knew that attracting his attention was the worse thing I could do. I held my breath, hoping he wouldn't damage the car too badly. I did not know why he was taking his rage out on the trunk of my car. I watched as he again raised himself to an erect position and plopped his paws on the car trunk with a loud thud. To my amazement the trunk door flew wide open.

I watched helplessly as he started checking out the inside of the trunk. Very slowly and calmly he reached into the trunk and pulled out a ham. It was then that I realized we hadn't gotten all of the groceries in the other day. The ham being frozen when we bought it and, all this while defrosting in the heat of the trunk and, the bear, obviously, picked up the scent.

We hadn't been the only ones watching the papa bear's antics with interest. Mama bear and baby bear sat quietly on their haunches waiting for the outcome too. Although they appeared interested in this new development, they didn't try to move closer to investigate.

Papa bear carefully caught the ham between his teeth and moved away from the car. Without a glance at his family, he began to devour the ham right before their eyes. Finally, just before it was all gone, he stopped eating and walked away, letting the mama and baby bear finish off what was left. He watched impatiently as they ate, and when they were done he carefully checked to see if they had left anything which he could nibble on. There was no doubt who the boss was in this family!

At last we realized, these bears weren't going to leave anytime soon. Our only recourse was to call the Department of Forestry and hope that they would come and rescue us, but that was not to be. The Department of Forestry simply told us to hold out a little while longer and the bears would go away by themselves.

We waited several more days and the bears were still with us. We called the Department of Forestry again. This time they told us they would be out in a day or so with some cages and would catch them, if they were still there. If they were still there!

Obviously, this trio had no intentions of ever leaving. They had plenty of apple trees to tear down for fruit, and now they were beginning to eat our chickens! There was still plenty of food around for them to continue to make pigs of themselves.

As we waited day in and day out to be released from our prison, we decided no one would really believe our story when it was over. We needed pictures. Very carefully, my friend crept up to the drapes and opened them just enough to stick the camera through. Suddenly she jumped back. The mama bear was only a few feet away. She looked up when she saw the drapes move and stared directly into my friend's eyes. The mama bear became instantly alert and began pawing the ground as though she were getting ready to charge.

My friend started crying, Lord have mercy. We have to run and hide. Hurry, hurry. As we started to scatter, I looked over my shoulder just in time to see the papa bear walk in front of the mama bear. She immediately quieted back down.

Thank God, I thought. *That papa bear sure is fantastic. Still, this isn't Goldilocks' three bears and I wish they would all go away.*

My friend cautiously moved toward the window to try taking their picture one more time. She was shaking so badly she couldn't hold the camera still.

She was afraid they would hear her snap the picture and charge her. I slowly got her to calm down, but it was to late.

After nearly two weeks, the bears had enough. Very slowly, papa bear started waddling off toward the woods. Mama and baby bear gradually followed. Their feet all moved in unison and it reminded me of a parade as they marched happily away keeping almost perfect time with one another. They certainly weren't Goldilocks' three bears. I wish they had been.

THE PORCUPINE WON

Our first three children were girls. We taught them to hunt and fish, but they preferred the more domestic side of life. We were not prepared, therefore, to handle the two rowdy boys that came along later. Although we tried to give them a well rounded education by teaching them to cook, sew, and even dance ballet, there was no way to hold them down.

As the boys grew older, they helped around the farm and enjoyed keeping busy. Whenever their chores were done, they would run off to go hunting in the forest that surrounded our home, or to go fishing or swimming in the river that cut through our property about a mile from our house.

One beautiful afternoon when the fall sun was shining warmly, Tim, who was thirteen, and Monte, who was eleven, finished their chores early and decided to catch some crawfish (or crawdads as we called them out West). After that, they would cool off swimming in the river. They rushed into the house to put on their swimming trunks, picked up a couple of buckets and towels and started off toward the river. As they ran, they called for their dog, Sheba, who galloped after them excitedly.

Around that time of year, the river was low and a person could easily walk across it in several spots, so I wasn't worried as I watched them trot off. I had a lot of chores to do myself that day and time flew by. Suddenly I became aware of the deepening shadows around me and wondered why the boys hadn't gotten home yet. I went inside to discover it was after 9:00 pm and began to worry. They had never stayed out so late before and were always home before dark. With my heart racing, I decided to follow the path to the river and try to find them.

At night in the dense forest it is extremely difficult to see where you are going. The deeper you get into the woods, the darker it becomes, and I was very much aware that I could get lost if I wandered too far.

The boys and I had a special signal that we used whenever I needed them. I would put my hands together just so and blow into them. The sound that emerged was loud and sounded a lot like a horn. Whenever they heard it they would answer in the same way. We would repeat our call, following the sound, until we came together. I tried it. There was no answer.

My mind began to race with fear. I pictured all the wild animals that roamed the forest at night cougars, black bears, coyotes, deer and raccoons, to name just a few. Even those animals that weren't predators could be dangerous if you surprised them. I tried to call over and over again with no answer, becoming more and more panicked with every passing minute.

I didn't know what to do. I was afraid that my calling out might attract the very animals I was concerned about, but I had to keep calling. Suddenly I stopped. Was that a noise? I held my breath and heard someone yelling. Soon I was hearing someone returning my horn call. Whoever it was kept coming closer and closer. I blew into my hand again as my heart raced. Soon I could hear someone running in the woods, yelling for me. Before long I saw Tim moving in leaps and bounds toward me. He was alone.

When he finally reached my side he was too breathless to speak. He kept trying to get words out, but he couldn't get a long enough breath. My heart was in my throat as I waited for his words. Had Monte been attacked by a bear or cougar? Had he drowned?

Finally, Tim got his breath back enough to tell me that Sheba had a run in with a porcupine. Her mouth was full of quills and Monte was with her. Monte had decided to take Sheba across the river to the nearby highway where he felt he could get help faster.

As Tim and I ran for home to get the car, he told me in gasping breaths more of the story. Sheba had fought with a porcupine and had lost. She had quills in her mouth and all over her jaw. They had rolled up a towel and put it to the back of Sheba's mouth so she couldn't close it, but the towel was too short to tie around her head and she wouldn't keep it in. She was in a great deal of pain and wouldn't let them carry her far. Monte had decided that their best bet was for him to ford the river, walk to the nearby highway and wait for us to pick them up in the car.

"Oh, Lord," I cried, "How ever will he find his way to the road in the dark carrying a squirming dog?" We jumped into the car and I tore out of the driveway, driving as fast as I dared around the curves in the road.

"Don't worry Mom," Tim said. "There is plenty of traffic on the highway. Monte will see the cars' lights and head toward them."

When we reached the other side of the river, I slowed down and traveled about three miles along the part of the road that I guessed to be behind our property. We didn't see a thing. I turned around and started tooting my horn as we moved slowly down the road again. After a while we got out of the car and shouted, listening for an answer to our calls. Nothing. We got back into the car and turned around again. This time I decided to try going a little farther down the road.

"Let me out of the car here, Mom," Tim said. Keep your bright lights on so I can see them and I'll head toward the river. You drive down the hill to see what you can find" I drove as close to the river as I could, then I got out of the car. I left the lights on and the motor running so Tim could find me. Soon he returned. He hadn't seen or heard any sign of Monte or the dog.

Once again we moved farther down the highway and stopped so Tim could look around. I stood by the car listening and yelling. Finally, I saw Tim running toward me waving his hands.

"Hurry, Mom," he yelled. "I think I hear him still farther down the road!"

We jumped back into the car and drove some more. Suddenly my headlights picked up the sight of a small boy and a dog on the side of the road. Monte had one hand holding the towel in Sheba's mouth and the other hand around her stomach. He was covered with mud and dirt, tears streamed down his face. What a beautiful sight! Tim and I jumped out of the car and ran to him. As soon as we reached Monte we grabbed him and hugged him so tight he could hardly breathe. We laughed and we cried with relief. Soon though, Sheba caught our attention and we looked at her helplessly. None of us had ever seen a porcupine before. We had no idea how to help her.

It was 11:30 pm by the time we got home. The nearest veterinarian was forty miles away and my old car couldn't make the trip. We brought Sheba into the house and tears filled our eyes as we saw her sorry state. She had more than thirty barbed quills sticking out of her tongue and jaw. We knew we had to try to get them out.

We got a pair of pliers and tried pulling one out. She yelped with pain. When we tried to pull out another one, she growled and wouldn't let us near her "This is much too painful for her," I said. "We have to figure out something to ease her suffering."

Suddenly I had an idea. It was a desperate plan, but maybe it would work. I ran to the phone and started dialing the number of the town doctor. It was after midnight now, but I had no qualms about waking him up. The phone on the other end rang about eight times before a sleepy voice answered. I quickly told him what had happened.

The doctor listened carefully and was extremely sympathetic. Perhaps being the only medical doctor for forty miles around, he was used to strange calls in the middle of the night. Whatever the reason, he accepted the call graciously. "It would probably be best to put the dog to sleep while you remove the quills," he said quietly. "I'll call the local pharmacist and prescribe a sedative for him."

"It's the middle of the night, doctor," I cried. "Do you think the pharmacist will drive to town at this time of night to fill a prescription for a dog?"

"Don't worry about it," he said. "I'll have him call you to tell you when you can meet him there."

I was amazed. Imagine living in a community where a medical doctor will prescribe a sedative for a dog and a pharmacist will travel miles into town in the middle of the night to fill it. It reminded me of the stories I had heard of the old time doctors who used to carry little black bags and make house calls. Sometimes living in a small community pays dividends you don't expect.

The pharmacist called and told us to meet him at his drug store at 1:30 am. When we got there he handed us the sedative and gave us careful instructions on how to administer it. We rushed home and carefully followed his instructions. It took Sheba a few minutes to doze off, but when she did, she didn't seem to feel a thing. A good thing too. It wasn't until much later that we were told that clipping off the ends of the quills with scissors allowed for their easier removal. We had pulled them out the hard way.

It took a while, but Sheba fully recovered from her ordeal. She had learned her lesson and never went near a porcupine again. I guess she knew the porcupine would always win!

About The Author

I was born in Birmingham, Alabama and grew up in North Carolina in a time the world was thrown into the Great Depression. Hunger gnawed at the stomachs of our family more often than not, even into near starvation. But along with this, came times of bonding together as a family and riding out the waves of life with a strong alliance to love and joy of being. This, through the years, taught us self-reliance and compassion.

In my lifetime, I have held several positions. One of the most memorable is being a mother. I feel other important positions I held were as a second class mechanic on airplanes during WW II and a teletypist for the Navy, relaying secret messages throughout the world. Now, at the end of my life, many things have brought on a reaping, a desire to relate to others my experiences in life.

www.ingramcontent.com/pod-product-compliance
Lightning Source LLC
Chambersburg PA
CBHW052246290526
45785CB00016B/1408